Better Homes and Gardens

HOUSE PLANTS

It's like dining *au jardin* year-round when the kitchen-family room includes a built-in planting pocket of this kind. Lush green plants and vines supply a constant background for flowering plants that can be changed with the different seasons.

Contents

Introduction

"To all who delight in the daily presence of green and growing things, this
book is dedicated. In it are advice and information for both the novice
and experienced gardener. Pictures and text show you how to select the right
plants...how to display them...how to keep them growing luxuriantly."

These words opened the introduction to the first edition of this book,
published 11 years ago. They continue to express the spirit and goals
that have directed the preparation of this new and completely revised edition.

Since the first book appeared, half a million readers have found it a reliable
guide, used its basic information to learn the whys and wherefores
of healthy house plants—how to light, water, feed, pot, and multiply them.
They have also profited from help that they received in finding
new ways to use plants decoratively—how to group them for mass effect and how
to position them singly to act as dramatic accents that serve
as importantly as do furnishings in bringing beauty to any room.

But in the 11 years since the first edition appeared, plant research has
produced much fresh information on many aspects of indoor
gardening. This has prompted the manufacture of new products—especially a
wide variety of equipment to aid gardening under lights and many
styles of prefabricated greenhouses that the homeowner can install himself.
Along with more knowledge and better equipment has come a
vastly expanded market of 'exotic plants,' varieties seldom seen in the past
outside a botanical garden. Today, 10-cent stores, supermarkets,
and plantsmen who specialize in mail orders, as well as your florist and
greenhouse, bring you fascinating plants from all over the
world to grow in your own home.

We are indebted to Kay Stroud for bringing all these new ideas, plants, and
equipment together in this, your guide to better living through
indoor gardening. You are invited to use these ideas through all the months
of the year for inspiration and guidance in growing plants
that will increase the beauty of your home and add pleasure to your daily life.

The Editors

Better Homes and Gardens

The large-leaved philodendrons of the vining type (some have leaves well over a foot long) make striking room accents when trained on a moss stick or a length of weathered wood.

◀ Palms at right, backed by podocarpus, philodendrons in foreground, and schefflera at left, which get light from clerestory window, are the major decorative motif for this room.

The Decorative Uses of House Plants

Plants are ornaments for the rooms in which you live. Of course, you enjoy them just for themselves, but you can increase your pleasure by selecting plants and placing them where they will be handsome room accents — the finishing touches to a decorating plan.

Perhaps you seek boldness of form or leaf pattern as a contrast to neutral backgrounds and solid colors. Or maybe color to reinforce the hues used in other furnishings is an important consideration. You may even wish to use a group of plants as a major decorative feature. Whatever you want done decoratively, there are plants to do it for you.

Depending on the size and style of the particular room, its colors, and the space available, consider whether you want to mass a number of plants in one impressive grouping or spotlight a single plant in a key location that makes it a focus of interest.

Think, too, in terms of scale. To decorate a large expanse of plain wall, you need a plant or group of plants large enough to blot out the empty look, but not so large that the once-empty wall seems overfilled.

Flowering plants in a kaleidoscope of hues can be the exclamation point in rooms that are furnished largely with furniture and accessories in neutral tones. Brilliant red azaleas, vivid yellow tulips, and pale blue hyacinths are excellent attention getters in a room of beige or a quiet white. No matter what type of setting you may have, nothing's a more effective color cure in the cold, winter months than a window garden full of bright, blooming plants.

But unless you can supply a location similar to the sun-filled corner pictured across the page (or have a home greenhouse), you'll probably have to settle for fewer plants in bloom and expand their impact by setting them among sturdy foliage plants.

This is a happy compromise if you shop wisely for flowering plants. Azaleas, cyclamen, or poinsettias purchased from your florist or greenhouse will stay in bloom for weeks, even months, if properly cared for. Choose plants with lots of buds, those not yet at their peak of color. Once in full bloom, position the plants so that they receive light but not full sun, which will push them rapidly to maturity and beyond. Cyclamen are an exception. They need full sun and ample water in order to go on blooming.

Installing a small light setup (see later section on gardening under lights) will provide you with the potential of blooming plants throughout winter that you can combine with faithful foliage performers. Many flowering favorites, such as geraniums and African violets, bloom repeatedly though not continuously indoors. If you rotate the plants, bringing those in bloom into view and placing those that have ended a period of bloom back under the lights, you'll increase greatly the color potential for your massed grouping of house plants.

Forcing spring-flowering bulbs is another way that you can flood your home with brilliant blooming plants—and at a small cost,

Here, a tall, elegant palm is attractively grouped with ferns and young schefflera. They're compatible in cultural needs and offer contrasts of foliage size and form.

too. Tulips, hyacinths, and daffodils can give you a late January-into-March bloom. (See the section on forcing bulbs for more information on this subject.)

For a wallop of color that will lift your spirits in midwinter, don't overlook that majestic bulb plant, the amaryllis. The cost of a cold-treated bulb (to bloom at Christmas during its first year) may run close to five dollars. Your original investment, however, can pay off in yearly bloom for many winters to come if you are willing to give the plant the necessary aftercare it needs for continued performance, as outlined on pages 56-57. Choose from velvet red, melting pink, coral and white as well as a large number of striped amaryllis varieties.

If you're an outdoor as well as an indoor gardener, don't overlook the many possibilities of lifting and potting some of the late-blooming garden plants, such as chrysanthemums and marigolds, to bring indoors before the first frost. If you wish to do so, make cuttings of such colorful foliage plants as coleus or waxy, red-leaf bedding begonias to root for indoor growth.

AVOID WATER DAMAGE
When you mass plants as suggested in this section, you improve greatly the conditions of humidity. Plants placed close together don't dry out as rapidly as those that are displayed singly or are sparsely grouped.

But you also introduce the problem of watering grouped plants without causing damage to room furnishings by water stains. You'll save watering time and potential damage to furnishings if you prepare carefully for your plant grouping in advance. You can do this in any one of several ways.

One excellent way is to use a built-in planter or area specially designed for growing plants, such as the one that is pictured on the first page of this chapter. It is not a difficult task to install a similar facility. Simply have a tinsmith fashion a shallow, waterproof metal tray of the proportions that you desire. Fill this tray in with pebbles and set your potted plants in place. Now, you can water freely—excess water will drain out satisfactorily, and you'll run little or no risk of water damage.

Mass plants for drama

For a coffee table or for a narrow shelf, choose a small gem that asks — and deserves — to be looked at closely. Just as an attractive ashtray or a colorful pillow can be a tasteful, decorative accent, so can small plants. They can pick up room colors, provide interesting contrast of form, and add attention-getting detail. But just as it would be wrong to expect a small accessory to carry a big decorative role in the home, so it would be a mistake to hope for big impact from a single small plant.

But a grouping of plants, many small, or one or two big plants, can carry important roles in a decorating scheme. The mass effect of a handsome grouping of plants has universal appeal. Any one plant in the group may be beautiful in its own right, though possible to overlook if alone. But put several plants together — in the right setting — and you can't possibly ignore their presence.

Of course, there's more than one way to group plants. A well-chosen pair is often just what you need to give a room that special touch. An assortment of many flowering varieties gives the same pleasure as looking into a florist's shop window. An all-foliage cluster, such as the one on the opposite page, is equally appealing.

Ideally, the area that you select for a dramatic display of plants should receive a good amount of natural light. If the daylight's inadequate, however, give preference to the setting that you have chosen and then consider what steps can be taken to reinforce natural light with artificial light. You can do this with ceiling spots, recessed light fixtures, or fluorescent tube lighting. (For more detailed suggestions on lighting, see 'Lighting' and 'Growing Plants Under Lights' in later sections of this book.)

It is also feasible, if your plant group is not too large, to install it on a mobile cart, taking it by day to a window location, then returning it after sundown to the room placement that you prefer.

Since plants grown indoors vary considerably in amounts of light required to promote good growth, you'll be wise to choose — for a dramatic grouping — varieties that have similar light needs. If the available natural light is low, choose plants from the group that can easily tolerate low light. If, on the other hand, your best location offers medium to strong light, select all of your plants for that kind of light.

To help you select from the right group, turn to the section entitled 'A Portfolio of Recommended House Plants,' in which plants are grouped according to the kind of light they need. (For additional information, also consult the plant lists on pages 88-89.)

Another important resource is your florist or greenhouse man. Besides supplying you with facts concerning light needs, he can give you a great deal of added information on plant cultural requirements (soil, water, humidity, etc.). From years of experience in the field, he will know which plants are cinch-to-grow types, and which are not.

After checking on compatibility of cultural needs, you'll want to seek contrasts of color, texture, and form within your group. Some of the greens vary from the palest chartreuse to almost black tones. Some plants have shiny foliage; others have a furry or velvety finish. There are also plants with big, pointed shaped leaves as well as rounded and pierced ones to choose from.

Get variety in size, too. Combine some tall and some short plants. Place taller ones toward the back; the shorter ones, forward. For a start, consider these combinations: a pot or two of small yellow chrysanthemums made to look still more flowery when backed by a good-sized dieffenbachia; or delicate ferns that take on the appearance of green lace if backed by the solid foliage of big-leaved philodendrons or rubber plants.

Clerestory lighting, as well as the large windows that admit bright light, offers excellent conditions for growing many flowering plants that add zest to a room's decorating scheme. ▶

Use one or two big plants as accents

Among the numerous revivals of yesterday's fashions in furnishings that are making news today is the hanging basket for plant display. Plants especially suited to growing in this manner include big, tropical-looking ferns such as the pair pictured on the opposite page, many vines such as English and kangaroo ivy, old-faithful philodendron, and ivy geraniums, as well as feathery-looking asparagus fern. All of these will thrive in bright light, and they welcome cooler temperatures found near a large window in wintertime if nighttime lows are not less than 65°.

PLANTS CONSIDERED AS OBJETS D'ART

The rapidly growing popularity of the home furnishings style known as eclectic—a planned mixture of old and new, combining furniture from a number of distinct periods in one scheme—also accounts for the return to favor of a number of house plants (like the fern) that had nearly disappeared from the home scene only a decade or two ago.

And with the return of the fern has come renewed popularity of hanging baskets, tall plant stands, and wicker ferneries, which were once featured in Victorian interiors. Today, it is the *style* of both plant and container that are sought after and appreciated. Properly treated, they are as much *objects d'art* as are paintings or sculpture.

In the room pictured across the page, the juxtaposition of the ultramodern lamp and functional shelving with a gracefully carved armoire offers a perfect setting for ferns in hanging baskets. Because of the choice of plants *and* the way they are dis-

played, they have become a major decorative feature of this interior.

The same plants can be used with quite a different effect if placed in another room and in containers of another style. Imagine, for instance, a room furnished with provincial pieces. Floor-based stands of wood or metal to blend with the other elements of the decor would make equally good use of this pair of ferns, but with an entirely different impact. Instead of the appealing antique flavor they carry in an eclectically furnished room, they would strengthen a mood of casual, homey comfort.

Again, in a formal directoire setting, on tall, fluted columns used as stands, the two ferns would heighten an air of opulence that is set by the other furnishings.

Consider, too, the possibilities of a wholly modern setting, a room where glass, chrome, leather upholstery, and predominantly neutral, unpatterned furnishings establish the bare look that is favored by many contemporary designers. A pair of large ferns, housed in a low planter of modern lines, inject a welcome contrast of free form to strict angular lines elsewhere prevalent in the room.

Learn to take advantage of plants and the way they are displayed to reinforce the mood of your favorite decorating style. Regardless of your style of furnishings, there are plants that will enhance your decor.

You can help to train your eye in the selection of the right plants and appropriate containers by studying the many kinds of interiors that are shown throughout this book. Watch for unusual ways to display plants, and use resourcefulness in modifying effects that you admire to suit the architectural and furnishings styles of your home. Resale shops, antique shops, auctions, and even your own attic or basement may possibly supply you with the raw material for ingenious stands and containers that help foliage and bloom to bring new life to any room.

◀ Boston ferns (*Nephrolepis*) need strong light and good humidity to keep fronds spring green. Hanging baskets are designed with built-in reservoirs, which make watering easy.

A luxury look comes easily and quickly to the rooms of your home when you invest in a suitable plant of larger size. In the room pictured across the page, the schefflera, which is the size of a young tree, is as important a decoration as the tall white screen that has been placed to offer a sharp, contrasting background for deep, glossy green foliage. As a living, growing decoration, it is doubly interesting.

If you are considering the use of a single, large, striking plant as a decoration in your home, you should study its placement just as carefully as you would that of any major piece of furniture. You want to make sure to locate your plant where it will not interfere with the normal traffic patterns, but where it will be seen easily from all parts of the room and recognized as important to the total decorating scheme. Make sure that there is enough space for the plant so that it will not look cramped, remembering also that it will continue to grow.

ASSESS THE AMOUNT OF LIGHT AVAILABLE

Having selected a location offering adequate space and a good background, the next step is to consider the amount of natural light available. The schefflera pictured at right is positioned next to a window. Filtered light coming through curtains is adequate since a schefflera does well in medium light and does not need full sun.

Should the ideal location for a big plant in your home be one deficient in daylight, your next consideration should be the possibility of supplementing natural light by installing fixtures for artificial light. Ceiling spots or recessed lighting directed toward the plant will probably be the solution if you choose a variety of plants that are tolerant of low light.

Among the varieties that you can expect to grow from two- to six-feet tall and that are tolerant of low to medium light are a number of palms, several varieties of dieffenbachia, the jade plant, and the Norfolk Island pine. In addition, many of the vining plants trained on moss sticks will grow tall and be bushy enough to fulfill the role of the important room accent. Several of the big leaf philodendrons, monstera, nephthytis, and grape ivy are good possibilities. All of these are pictured elsewhere in this book.

LEARN PROPER CARE

First, acquaint yourself thoroughly with the cultural requirements of the plant you've chosen—needed amounts of water, fertilizer (don't overdo), and humidity. In later sections, you'll find cultural information on all of the large plants that have been mentioned here as well as photographs and growing hints on many others.

Then, set yourself a conscientious schedule for attending to your plant's needs. Actually, they'll be less than those required by the small plants, since big pots dry out at a slower rate than do little ones.

Until you establish a pattern for watering, always dig down with small trowel or spoon to see if the soil two or three inches below the surface is dry. In a big pot, the topsoil may be very dry, but the soil only a few inches down can be quite moist. Since the bulk of roots are in the bottom half of the pot, they can rot if watered excessively.

USING PERMANENT PLANTS

There are some home locations where you despair of keeping a large—and expensive—plant growing healthily, yet you want that lavish accent, which only a big plant can supply. An entrance hall lacking in natural light and subject to drafts of opening and closing doors is a typical problem location.

Before you choose a big, man-made plant for such a situation, visit a greenhouse or nearby public conservatory. Look with careful attention at appearance of bark, leaf texture, and differences in tones of the new versus the older foliage. You'll be prepared in this way to judge the quality of a skillfully fabricated permanent plant, for it should duplicate the natural features that you've observed in the living plant you like.

This flourishing schefflera looks right in its ▶ shining metal container, which is big enough to give the plant a stable, well-balanced appearance. Its demands for care are modest.

Let plants augment a room's decorating scheme

Almost any green or flowering plant is a welcome, fresh accent in almost any room—in the kitchen, dining or living room, or bedroom. But a good choice of plants together with the right size and color container can do more, decoratively speaking.

For example, flowering plants whose blooms pick up the hues used in the furnishings (as do the red geraniums in the room pictured across the page) become an integral part of a total color scheme. By placing the plants in those parts of the room where you wish to reinforce an accent color, you can often achieve an effect that would be difficult to accomplish in other ways. The difficulty lies in sustaining this color accent throughout the year.

Inviting as it is to think of using flowering plants keyed to a color scheme, there are factors of cost and time to consider. If you have a small greenhouse or a light setup, you have the facilities for forcing spring-flowering bulbs. Using these conveniences, it is possible to substitute time for money and to know the luxury of living with flowering plants through many months of the year at a relatively small expense. If you must purchase all blooming plants, the cost (though worth it in the returns of excitement) may be greater than your present budget permits. It is an unfortunate fact that most blooming plants do not remain continuously in bloom. Although many carry on for weeks, even months, practically none can be counted on to bloom freely year-round.

More subtle (and more enduring) than color is the choice of a plant or group of plants to advance the theme of style. Although the majority of those plants we think of as house plants are, botanically speaking, *exotic* (not native to our climate) some of them look the part far more so than do others. The dracaena pictured on the facing page, with its stark stems and bursts of foliage at branch tips, is such a plant. It has the air of belonging to its setting, with color and form related to the patterned fabric and terrazzo flooring associated with Mediterranean style.

It is a native of the Canary Islands, just off the North African coast, close by the Mediterranean, so its appropriate look is not purely accidental. Its placement, against the expanse of white curtain, gives it a setting that capitalizes on interesting form.

Other plants that might have been used effectively in this same setting—taking into account the amount of light available—include the large specimens of Norfolk Island pine, schefflera, rubber plant, several of the palms that can be counted on to reach a height of five or six feet, and a monstera trained on a tall moss stick. All of these grow well in a filtered light situation—providing there is sufficient humidity in the immediate surroundings—either naturally available or in the form of artificial light supplied by you in supplementary amounts during the cold winter and early spring months.

CONTAINERS ARE IMPORTANT
The large black container on a footed base plays an indispensable role and contributes to the decorative importance of the dracaena pictured opposite. Its color is coordinated with the room's decorating scheme, and its shape and bulk convey a sense of solidity that is necessary for large foliage plants.

So when choosing house plants to augment your decorating scheme, take the color, style, and form of the container and of the plant into consideration.

◀ *Dracaena Draco*, often called 'Dragon Tree.' is available in several varieties. All make attractive pot plants and prefer temperatures under 70 and 30 percent humidity.

Window walls of modern apartments invite you to capitalize on the decorative uses of house plants (top). Have a greenhouse atmosphere with a citrus tree (lemon, left) and a *Dracaena fragrans* (reflected in mirror).

Take a cue from museums of art that recognize the affinity of plants and modern paintings. They're paired most harmoniously when scale of plants and pictures is similar.

The grace and drama of floor-to-ceiling windows in a traditionally furnished living room are decoratively reinforced by the placement of a camellia trained to grow to tree height, with a setting of ferns spotted at its base. ▶

20

WINDOWS ARE SHOWCASES FOR HOUSE PLANTS

Take a tip from jewelers who know how to display their gems effectively—in brightly lighted windows. Plants, too, sparkle when they're set in the showcase of your windows. Light makes the colors of bloom and foliage all the more glowing, and it is good for a plant's growth (provided you choose in accordance with specific plant requirements).

A window garden can be part of the architecture, as it is in the case of the dining room pictured on this page, and the kitchen opposite. It can also be assembled by placing plants on stands in front of a window or by installing a hanger such as that in the family room, where an old scale helps suspend a fern in front of a window.

The most successful window garden—whether it includes one or a score of plants—is one planned to suit the plants that it features in respect to light, temperature, and humidity. If you have a south window, you can grow a variety of flowering plants. East and west windows, too, get enough sun to please some of the most attractive members of the foliage plant family as well as a number of favorite flowering varieties.

In a window garden that features a wide variety of grouped plants, prepare for it in advance by installing shallow plant trays of waterproof metal or plastic. Fill trays to a depth of an inch or more with pebbles. After making sure that all clay pots that can be seen are scrubbed and clean, you're ready to set the plants on display. Since all excess water can drain off into the pebbles beneath pots, and add humidity to the air, watering chores are greatly reduced and problems of overwatering are solved.

For a hanging garden effect, set pots on a saucer that allows for water to drain off, or into a metal or ceramic container that will prevent damage to furnishings.

Depending on the amount of light and the exposure of the window or windows you're using as plant showcases, consult chapters on both foliage and flowering plants as well as the portfolio section for help in selecting the most suitable varieties. Consider, too, the possibilities of installing a window greenhouse as discussed on pages 69-85.

An army of healthy young ferns marches smartly across two shelves of a recessed dining room window (top). They're set onto trays to make watering easy. Luxuriant gloxinias on dining table echo a handsome rug pattern.

Repeating color of cabinets and counters (top right) are bright geraniums massed in a kitchen window. Keep plants from growing leggy by pinching back tall branches, and avoid overwatering to get more continuous bloom.

This display technique for a hanging fern is geared to a provincial decor (bottom right). Masses of bloom on a calceolaria (pocketbook plant) augment red in tableware and upholstery fabric, advancing a total color scheme.

PLANTS AND ARCHITECTURE

Besides the use of house plants to augment the color and style of furnishings, they also can carry an important role as complements to the lines of modern architecture. Against a simple background for living, plants can introduce contrasting decorative forms that add visual excitement.

Living plants, as well as paintings and sculpture, can subtly soften and also increase the appeal of geometrically designed interiors. The room settings pictured on these pages testify to this.

To make certain that plants will be used and placed for the best possible effect, an architect frequently builds a planter into the house, indicating where plants should be placed to complement the clean, straight lines of the interior. The sculptured look of big foliage plants—or a grouping of large and small ones—is nowhere more striking and appropriate than in such a setting. Leaf patterns seen against the sweep of a plain wall or next to the rough texture and rectangular pattern of interior brick become far more than a decorative afterthought.

In such settings, scale is a prime consideration. Notice that, in the room pictured at the top of the   this page incorporating

A free-form metal tray fashioned to encircle a pillar in this apartment living room allows easy maintenance of massed plants. The plants introduce, through foliage patterns, welcome contrast to an unadorned setting.

Countering the simplicity of glass and brick and vinyl flooring, which are the major architectural ingredients of this room, foliage and flowering plants, placed at varied levels, inject needed color, detail, and pattern.

one tall plant is vital to the success of the entire grouping. Without this plant, the relationship between the massed plants and the big column at whose foot they are placed would be unsatisfactory.

In the rooms that are shown on this page, the need for plant height is reduced, but there must be some specimens in each group whose leaves are large enough to be seen and enjoyed at a distance. If all of the plants were fine-leaved, the groupings could not have the same importance in relation to their architectural setting.

For all interior plantings, unless they are next to windows that admit sufficient light, it is necessary to arrange for artificial lighting to keep plants healthy.

ESTABLISH A SCHEDULE FOR GROOMING

As significant as the proper choice of plants in regard to scale, contrast, and location is good grooming. Does the foliage look dusty? It's a good practice to carry a soft, dampened cloth with you whenever you water your plants. Wipe the leaves gently, supporting each leaf while you are dusting it. Also, remove the yellowing foliage for tidy, well-tended plant appearance.

Innovative design for a built-in planter admits light at floor level (top). Tall form and large leaves of the monstera, given center placement, supply focus for the grouping of foliage plants, mostly feathery foliage types.

Footed plant stands in staggered arrangement secure variation in plant height for grouping. Flowering plants spotted forward can be changed seasonally, but foliage plants will continue in place as a green background.

Shining foliage of varied leaf patterns contribute to the appeal of interior brick and quarried tile flooring in a contemporary setting (left). An edging of crushed marble chips underscores flowing form of planter itself.

Commercially sold as an aralia, this graceful, fine-leaved plant is the *Dizygotheca elegantissima*. It requires medium light and average humidity (30 percent) for good growth.

◀ *Ficus elastica* (left) and *Ficus pandurata* have similar needs, as outlined in text at right. Bird's-nest fern, *Asplenium nidus* (lower right), needs soil rich in leaf mold and peat moss, and good humidity. (See also page 41.)

Favorite Foliage Plants

Green is a color you never tire of—restful to the eye and refreshing to the spirit. That is one reason why foliage plants are so popular. Indoors, in winter, green leaves hint of springtime to come; in summer, they look cool and woodsy when temperatures soar.

You can't possibly grow all the desirable foliage plants there are. Use pictures and cultural information here, as well as in the portfolio section, to choose those plants having the qualities you admire.

Size is a prime factor in your choice of house plants, so begin by considering some of the big, handsome varieties that can hold their own in decorative roles. The India rubber tree, for example, pictured far left across the page, is probably the most popular of all large house plants. Its big, shiny leaves offer good contrast to the textures of other home furnishings. And it requires only minimal care. Both the rubber tree and its relative, the fiddle-leaf fig, at its right, tolerate medium light and average house humidity quite well. Their only real enemy is overwatering, which will cause root rot.

26

THE LUXURY LOOK

The luxury look comes easily and quickly to the rooms of your home when you invest in suitable plants of larger size. If time is not important, however, you can begin with young ones and enjoy them as they grow.

All of the large plants on these pages—dieffenbachia on this page, monstera and devil's ivy opposite (grown totem style)—prefer filtered light to full sun. All three are large enough to look right placed on the floor or near a wall or a window.

Big plants like these need some space around them and large containers so that they'll have a well-balanced, stable appearance. As far as daily care is concerned, they make only modest demands.

For these—and all large plants grown in big pots—the most frequent cause of failure is overwatering. A check of surface soil is not adequate. You'll have to dig down with spoon or trowel to see whether the soil at the outer edge of the pot at a depth of two or three inches is dry. If it's dry, it's time to water. If it's moist, however, the soil at the center of the container has ample moisture to feed the main root mass, which is located in the middle of the container. In a month or two (allowing for some differences between cold and warm weather rates of evaporation) you'll know, approximately, how often a given plant needs watering.

Plants with vining tendencies are among the most popular foliage plants. They are exceptionally easy to grow in the home, and they're within everyone's budget if they are purchased as young plants and brought to the desired height over a period of time.

There are two ways of training such vining plants: **1.** on a moss stick, as sketched at the bottom of the opposite page; and **2.** on a length of bark-covered wood or of pressed fern (osmunda) fiber, which you can buy from a garden center shop. The moss stick is superior since it permits you to pour water into the central cylinder as well as into the pot, thereby providing a moist growing medium for the aerial roots that the plant will produce. This method allows you to supply water not only to roots at the base but all the way to the top, where it's also necessary for healthy plant growth.

Aristocratic monstera, native to South America, adapts well to home growing conditions. It tolerates any exposure but direct sun. Grows best in a moist atmosphere, which you can provide by pouring water into top of moss stick support.

◄ Young plants of *Dieffenbachia rudolph roehrs* (one of some 30 varieties of this plant) have an attractive chartreuse tint. Old plants that go leggy can be brought back to earth by the process of air-layering. (See last chapter.)

Devil's ivy (mistakenly called variegated philodendron) grows more slowly than common philodendron, which also does well on a moss stick. It needs stronger light than monstera in order to retain the white splashes in leaves.

Stuff hardware cloth column with sphagnum moss. Set into deep pot; fill with soil.

One of the most common varieties of dracaenas, *D. massangeana*, wins enthusiastic praise for its glossy foliage. A light green stripe runs down the center of each long leaf. If the leaf tips become brown, it's usually a sign of improper watering—too little or too much produces symptom. Good drainage and a potting mixture that retains moisture are solutions.

This variety of fig—Celeste—lends itself to pot culture if you add dolomitic lime once a year to sweeten soil. It's deciduous, so leaves drop in fall, but angular stems have rugged beauty. Water lightly while it's dormant.

Dracaena janet craig (below) has several relatives of similar appearance, and all are often called 'dragon trees.' They do well in medium light and average house humidity if grown in porous soil and provided with good drainage.

RUGGED GOOD LOOKS

In an informal setting, foliage plants with a tailored look are good decorative choices. The three pictured on these pages have that quality and would look perfectly at home in a den, family room, or study. All are large enough to be used as the focal point for a mass arrangement of plants.

Two are dracaenas—the one at the left and the one across the page. Explore this family and you'll discover tremendous variety in size and leaf pattern. Dracaenas thrive in moist soil, but prefer a warm temperature.

The fig, above, is a fruit-bearing tree that's a bit unusual grown in a container. It is handsome from spring through fall.

Begonias for year-round performance

Grown more for foliage than for flowers, the begonia family is among the most satisfying of house plants. The leaves remain attractive year-round, and if you give begonias bright light, they will bloom in winter.

Of the three major categories of begonias, the rhizomatous and fibrous are most often grown as house plants. Sketches of leaf types at right give you some notion of the numerous variations that are obtainable. Tuberous begonias (see page 35) can be cultivated as house plants, too, but they're most often seen in hanging baskets on a porch, or planted out in shaded flower beds.

Rex begonias, two examples of which are pictured across the page, are usually rhizomatous but are often considered a separate class because their jewel-toned foliage demands more warmth and greater humidity than do other kinds of rhizomatous begonias.

While begonias appreciate humidity, they do not like the soil that is constantly moist. Don't water them until the topsoil is dry to the touch. Also, make certain that excess water can drain out of the pot.

During the winter, begonias need a lot of sunlight; indirect but bright light is best the rest of the year, for the foliage will pale if the sun is too brilliant. They grow best in 65° to 70° temperatures.

TAKE PRECAUTIONS WHEN POTTING BEGONIAS

When potting begonias, set each plant with its crown barely above the soil and not in a depression where water can collect. The soil should be porous and slightly acid—containing some peat moss and leaf mold.

◄ Rex begonias (in foreground) have vivid foliage. Although hard to grow in average home humidity, they do well under lights. The tall plant, Ruth Grant, is a fibrous begonia.

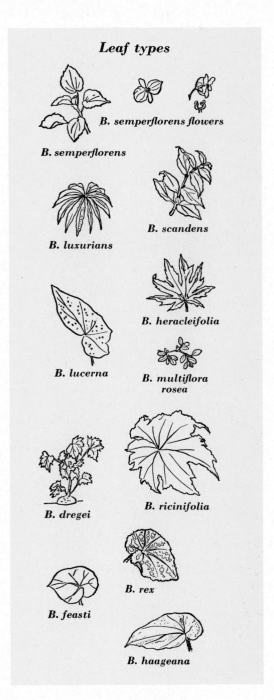

Leaf types

B. semperflorens flowers

B. semperflorens

B. scandens

B. luxurians

B. heracleifolia

B. lucerna

B. multiflora rosea

B. dregei

B. ricinifolia

B. rex

B. feasti

B. haageana

The angel-wing begonias (top left) are especially generous with winter bloom. This one, Robinson's peach, is typical of the group's growth pattern, with leaf nodes occurring at wide intervals on the thick stems.

The young Rex begonia plant (bottom) has gemlike violets and blue reds mixed with green in foliage that fit almost any decorating color scheme. During the summer, they're easy to grow. In winter, they need high humidity.

This distinctively patterned Rex (iron cross) is unusual also for its deeply veined foliage, which gives it a seersucker look. For information on growing this — and others of the Rex group — see 'Gardening under Lights.'

Recent begonia introductions include a wide ▶ range of smaller foliaged types (such as the lower two pictured opposite), backed by the beefsteak begonia — a standard and favorite member of the rhizomatous group, with glossy green top and red underleaf. Note the difference in size of the newer varieties in foreground.

The most common type of fibrous begonia is *B. semperflorens*. The blooms of these begonias range from white through pale pink, coral, and red, and the foliage colors vary from bright green to bronzy and a dark blood red. The newer fibrous begonia varieties have semidouble as well as double flowers that resemble tiny rosebuds.

For continued bloom, these begonias need a sunny window, a standard potting soil mixture, ample water (when you water), and good drainage. You can have more plants by cutting back the tall branches and rooting them. Pictures and text at left tell how.

Use a knife to make 3- to 4-inch cuttings from mature plant (top left). Make cut on a slant. Pinch off or cut away enough of the lower leaves to allow for inserting the cutting one or two inches deep in rooting medium.

Fill a shallow container (top right) with coarse sand, perlite, or vermiculite, and moisten rooting medium, making sure that excess water drains off. Use pencil to poke holes, then insert cuttings one or two inches deep.

When cuttings (lower left) have developed roots an inch long (in two or three weeks), it's time to pot each one in a 2- or 3-inch clay pot. Supply bottom drainage with pebbles or potsherds. Water well after potting.

In a few weeks, plant roots should fill soil of a small pot. Check (lower right) by tapping the pot against a table while supporting plant with other hand. If well rooted, shift to larger pot or group several in one large pot.

For an important wall decoration, group a number of small begonias in a wall tree with a big ceramic container at the base, planted to give a full, bushy look.

Healthy, small tubers will flower, but bigger ones send up more stems. For most spectacular bloom size, select tubers that measure about 1½ inches across. Blooms of the bush type are larger than are hanging-basket types.

Use 6- to 7-inch pots when planting tubers. Fill almost to rim with potting soil rich in leaf mold and sphagnum moss. Press rounded side of tuber into moist soil. Don't cover dished-in top until sprouts are three inches tall.

Suspend tuberous begonias of pendulous type in a hanging basket (above). Make sure that they don't get full sun in the middle of the day, and protect them from strong winds.

TUBEROUS BEGONIAS

To brighten up a porch or a patio that is protected from direct sun, why not select one or more tuberous begonias? Their requirement of partial shade makes them ideal choices for pots and hanging baskets.

Flower sizes run from two to as much as eight inches in width. In shape, some resemble rosebuds, carnations, or the smooth semi-double and double camellias. Others remind you of giant crape-myrtle blooms. All but the Picotee type, which have deeper color in the margins of petals, are in solid colors.

Partial shade, a loose, rich soil, protection from wind, and moisture in both air and soil are the four requirements for success.

Tubers that are started in very early spring can be enjoyed as house plants for several weeks before you set them outdoors. When the blooming period is over, the tubers can be dried out, stored in plastic bags in a cool spot, and saved. The following year you can plant them again (as shown at right).

Saxifraga sarmentosa is this plant's botanical name. It's also called strawberry begonia and strawberry geranium, though strawberry saxifrage is a more accurate label for this newer variety named 'Magic Carpet.' It needs medium to bright light and rich, moist soil.

Start caladium tubers (above) in wet peat moss or sand. Roots grow from tops of tubers. After they've sprouted, repot; place tubers an inch below soil surface. This size plant can be grown in six to eight weeks.

Another variety of caladium (left) has green veining on white leaves. These plants need warmth—70° minimum. When new growth ceases, stop watering. Rest and dry tubers till next season. Store in plastic bags in cool spot.

Foliage plants in flower colors

If you've always thought of foliage plants as green, you're in for a nice surprise. Gay-as-a-rainbow foliage is not as rare as you may think. Some kinds are seasonal, like the fancy-leaf caladium in shadings of pink, red, and white with green. This particular variety grows from tubers indoors in cold weather, in shaded spots outdoors in summer. Others, like coleus (top right), are year-rounders. Your florist or greenhouse man sells short, bushy plants each spring to set into outdoor flower beds and borders. But you can have these plants indoors, too; they're quite easy to root from stem cuttings, and they will grow willingly from seed. Choose from a wide variety of reds, yellows, and oranges, with or without a mixture of green in the ruffle-edged leaves.

Crotons (bottom right) are grown as shrubs in the deep south, as house plants elsewhere. They do demand high humidity, however, so you may have to supplement the moisture in your home during the winter months.

Among other colorful foliage plants not pictured here are begonias, velvet plant, calathea, episcia (also called flame violet), red-nerved fittonia, some of the tradescantias, maranta, *Cissus discolor,* and several of the 'fancy-leaf' geraniums, as well as Joseph's coat *(Alternanthera).* For further information on many of these foliage plants, consult the index for page numbers.

In general (there are a few exceptions), the more colorful the foliage, the brighter the indoor light a plant requires in order to maintain its most brilliant display. It won't take you very long to find out if the sun is insufficient, as the colors in new foliage will be paler—or absent.

What constitutes the proper amount of light for a given variety of plant is a question many beginners find puzzling. Once you realize that the brightest winter sun indoors is but a tiny fraction in strength of full sunlight outdoors in summer, this will help you understand house plant requirements. For more information on varying light needs, consult section entitled 'Light.'

Ever-willing coleus (top) can be kept young, short, and perky by rooting tips (three to four inches long) in soil or water when stems get overly tall. Colors are most brilliant when they receive some sunlight each day.

Splashed with gold, red, and green, the curious croton grows leaves of many different colors on one plant. Regard these plants as cut flowers unless you can supply high humidity (over 50 percent); discard when unattractive.

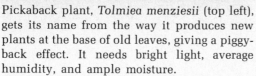

Pickaback plant, *Tolmiea menziesii* (top left), gets its name from the way it produces new plants at the base of old leaves, giving a piggy-back effect. It needs bright light, average humidity, and ample moisture.

Pair two kinds of succulents (top right) for plants that resemble sculpture: rosettes of echeveria and lanky euphorbias. In general, the succulents tolerate low humidity. (See pages 44-47 for more information.)

White-veined fittonia is not a rugged plant, but ▶ its appearance is quite handsome. To provide the humid air that it requires, keep a clear plastic cake cover over the plant most of the time or grow it in a terrarium.

Small gems—worth a close-up

If your home is small and limited in windows suitable for growing plants, the group pictured here should interest you. None of these plants grow large in average home conditions, and all have remarkable foliage—interesting for its pattern, color, or form.

Give any of these top billing by placing them where they can be enjoyed close at hand. In addition to their appeal as living, growing examples of nature's artistry, they'll serve as valuable a decorative role as might some far more costly *objet d'art.*

Because they're small, it's an easy task to shift them from more congenial daytime locations (insofar as healthy growth is concerned) to a tabletop, where a pool of lamplight can focus attention on subtle foliage patterns or curious habits of growth.

The maranta, or prayer plant, which gets its common name from its habit of folding up its leaves at night, will work overtime under lamplight, which dramatizes the striking foliage. By day, it likes medium light and soil rich in organic material to keep the roots moist.

Ferns for all seasons

Over the years, the Boston fern has been the most popular member of the *Nephrolepis* family, even though scores of related varieties have been developed commercially. This is largely due to its accommodating ways and lacy good looks, which recommend it as a house plant. Demands are quite specific: bright light (not sun); soil rich in organic material (half sphagnum moss); frequent watering; and good drainage. Given these, ferns will reward you with vigorous growth.

If the Boston fern that you bought in spring or summer turns brown and ceases to put forth new fronds when winter comes, you've probably not taken into account the much higher rate of evaporation when the central heating robs the air of its humidity. The plant can get along well with average humidity, but it needs frequent watering.

FERNS COME FROM MANY PLANT FAMILIES

Asplenium is another plant family from which a number of handsome ferns come, including the bird's-nest fern (below). Its leaves are whole rather than feathery, and it prefers more humidity than does the Boston fern; otherwise, it takes the same conditions.

Whitman, curly, crested—these are a few of the names by which the more finely divided varieties of the Boston fern are known. They are slow growing, but need the same culture.

Asplenium nidus (right) needs ample moisture at the roots, but it will turn brown in winter in high humidity. Plant does best in cool house temperatures, not over 70° in winter.

◀ The bright light of a window wall is ideal for a Boston fern *(Nephrolepis bostoniensis)*. It is easy to grow new plants from runners. (See last chapter for information on propagation.)

A lovely, curving branch of driftwood (top right) adds grace to the beauty of English ivy as it supports the vine. Help the plant get established by securing it to the wood with green florists' tape or foliage-green yarn.

Monstera's exotic look (bottom left) makes it popular as an accent for contemporary interiors. New leaves won't be deeply split unless plant gets medium light. Any plant this big is costly, so start with a small one.

Emerald Gem (bottom right), is the commercial name under which this variety of *Nephthytis* is sold. Easy to grow, it likes ordinary temperatures and tolerates low light. It gets stringy if grown too long in a dark spot.

Vining plants for varied foliage patterns

To show off vining and trailing plants to best advantage, place them where the softening effects of their natural growth habits will look appropriate. Younger, smaller specimens take to tables, window ledges, shelves, and plant boxes where they can spill gracefully over the edge and follow their normal inclinations. Older, larger plants, if too big for such placement, can be trained on a variety of supports, such as moss sticks or trellises, where they can send growth upward or—like the ivy at left—follow the interesting curves of driftwood.

In addition to placement where they show off as individuals, the large, vining plants can serve as handsome background greenery for a massed indoor planting of the sort that is pictured in the first chapter. They can, indeed, play a major role in such an arrangement, for most of the other foliage plants will be low, bushy, and in need of tall contrast for a dramatic effect.

Even the most inexperienced of indoor gardeners are familiar with English ivy and the common or heartleaf philodendron as examples of vining plants. But even 'old hands' may be unaware of the tremendous variety available and the unusual effects that can be gained from some of the less-familiar members of the vining tribe.

A large number of the vining plants, which you may know only from seeing them grow freely in a native tropical or subtropical climate, are easily adaptable to pot culture. Bougainvillea, star jasmine, passion-flower, hoya, and stephanotis are but a few of the many vining plants that can be grown as house plants and that—in season—favor you with colorful or fragrant bloom, as well as perennially pleasing foliage. You'll need to provide all of these plants with higher humidity (50 percent) during the cold, winter months. When summer comes, a shady, outdoor location will keep them healthy until cold weather makes its appearance.

Waxy blooms of stephanotis are prized for fragrance—they are used in bridal bouquets. Grow outdoors in summer; bring indoors before frost and water less often so the plant goes semidormant. Grow in bright light.

44

Called 'chin cactus' (left) because of the protuberances below each cluster of spines, which are reminiscent of a double chin, *Gymnocalycium michanovichii* is easy to grow. The large blooms are long lasting. Allow the sandy soil mixture (half sand and half good garden loam) to become quite dry between waterings. Grow in medium to bright light.

Brown-pointed markings on its leaves make *Kalanchoe tomentosa* or panda plant, as it's commonly called (below), attractive to grow as a house plant. As it grows older, it puts out side branches in a bushy growth pattern. Scientific species name, *tomentosa*, indicates that the leaves are covered with a dense matting of hairs, giving a furry look.

Cotyledon undulata (above) is a well-branched variety of succulent with wavy edges on up-curved leaves, which are covered with a thick, waxy white bloom that rubs off when the plant is handled. The mature plant reaches a height of three feet and bears orange-colored flowers during the summer. Some 30 species of this family have been identified.

Lithops loucheana (right) is the botanical name of this odd little succulent, much like the 50-some other varieties of this plant family— all native to South Africa. The plant consists of leaves in pairs, split by a central fissure from which flowers emerge. Lithops usually grow in clumps. The name, 'lithops,' refers to the rocklike appearance of this succulent.

Cactus and succulents to grow indoors

All cactus plants are succulents, although the reverse is not true. There are nearly 30 separate groups of plants that include succulent varieties, the cactus being but one of the tribe. And since it's not always easy to be absolutely certain which thorny and prickly plants are true cactus, it's safest to refer to them all as 'succulents.'

The ability to store water is a trait common to all succulents. You'll understand this if you study the diagram and text below and at left to see how they're made.

Virtually all succulents thrive indoors in a soil mixture that's half sand and half good garden loam. They withstand low humidity and prefer medium to bright light.

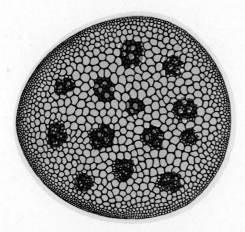

Slightly waxy outer skin, almost impervious to water and gases, covers leaves and stems as shown in enlarged cross section of a stem.

Small, hard-walled cells are a barrier to escape of water from big, thin-walled cells that are inner reservoirs of food and water.

Water tubes are scattered throughout mass of inner cells, several to a bundle. They conduct water taken in by roots through the plant.

Tubes carrying food run alongside water tubes but conduct in both directions, letting succulents live on reserves between rains.

Globular in shape, *Echinocactus grusonii*, along with a number of other related varieties, is often called 'barrel cactus.' It is a native of the mountains of Mexico and eventually grows to a size much too large for indoor culture. But in its juvenile stage, it is an especially easy one to grow as a house plant. When in bloom, the flowers are red and yellow.

The tall plant is *Crassula arborescens;* leaning out right is *Crassula perforata. Sedum adolphii* and echeveria are rosette shapes. These succulents require medium light and soil that's half sand and half garden loam.

The main caution for succulent-cactus dish gardens—don't overwater. Tallest plant, *Opuntia leucotricha;* in front of it, *Stapelia nobilis.* Small cacti at left, *Mammillaria kewensis* (front) and *Cleistocactus straussii* (rear).

Little gardens to grow in a dish

Green gardens that grow in a dish are fun to plant and pretty to look at. They are attractive as table centerpieces, or as decorations for an end table, buffet, or chest.

First, decide where the dish garden is to be placed on display. If it's to be seen from all sides rather than viewed mostly from the front, plant it accordingly.

Select young foliage plants that contrast pleasantly with each other. Include a variety of heights, leaf shapes, sizes, textures, and patterns. Combine only plants having similar light and water needs.

Your container can be as simple or as elegant as you like—metal, ceramic, or plastic—in keeping with its surroundings. But don't use a container that is too shallow. Make sure to allow for a bottom layer of pebbles plus soil. Most plants need at least three inches of depth for stability and root growth.

Cover bottom of container (top left) with a layer of pebbles, gravel, charcoal, or broken clay pots for drainage. Next, add a layer of standard potting soil—equal parts of gravel, garden loam, and peat or leaf mold.

Before setting plants in place (top right), try out your arrangement for attractiveness. Place the tall plants in the back and center—or slightly off-center; the shorter ones at the front and sides. Firm soil. Water.

These plants (right) tolerate low light: Chinese evergreen (tall plant in center); at its left, *Dracaena sanderiana*; at right, *Dracaena godseffiana*; and in front of it, *Peperomia obtusifolia variegata*. Vine is devil's ivy.

Terrariums

Like an oasis in a desert, a tiny garden growing inside a glass container has an irresistible fascination. A terrarium invites you to paint your own scene, imitating nature on a miniature scale.

The dry, hot air of the house in winter is no handicap to plants in a terrarium, where moist air is trapped. Since the moisture is so well conserved, your garden under glass will hardly ever need watering.

TIPS ON PREPARING AND PLANTING

Wash and polish the container so that it sparkles. Then, layer charcoal, gravel, and soil—see diagram at the bottom of the page. For an extra touch, put down a first lining layer of moss with its green side out.

A good soil mixture for terrariums is 2 parts loam, 2 parts coarse sand, and 1 part leaf mold—not so rich in organic material that plants will rapidly outgrow limited space.

Before planting the terrarium, decide where you are going to display it. If it's to be seen from one side, put the larger plants in back; smaller ones in front. If it will be seen from all sides, center the bigger ones and surround them with smaller ones.

The trickiest step is the initial watering. Moisten the soil (don't drench it, as you'll be plagued with mold). If you're doubtful about the right amount of water, stay on the dry side, for you can always add moisture if foliage shows signs of wilting.

Use the glass lid to control humidity. If moisture regularly condenses in noticeable amounts, remove cover for a day or leave it partly open until excess moisture disappears. Place your glass garden in good light, but not in full sun, for this will trap too much heat and kill the plants.

◀ A wide-mouth glass jar on a stand makes an unusual display case for a terrarium planted with small ferns and woodland plants, with red partridge berries as a focal point.

Not all plants are suited to terrariums. The high humidity would cause some to decay. The best plants are those native to woodlands and marshy places. Listed below are some plants that need humidity, grow slowly, and help to create an interesting terrarium. Most must be ordered from plantsmen specializing in wild flowers.

Recommended for closed terrariums are ferns of small size, such as *Polypodium vulgare,* maidenhair *(Adiantum pedatum)* and *Pteris* (table ferns); mosses of almost every sort; trailing arbutus *(Epigaea repens)*, rattlesnake plantain *(Goodyera pubescens)*; common and striped pipsissewas *(Chimaphila)*; wintergreen *(Pyrola elliptica)*; goldthread *(Coptis trifolia)*; hepatica; small yellow ladyslipper *(Cypripedium parviflorum)*; and partridge-berry *(Mitchella repens).* Several of the insectivorous plants are also good terrarium specimens.

(1) Charcoal base keeps soil sweet; **(2)** 1 inch of gravel provides drainage; and **(3)** sufficient soil holds roots. **(4)** Line outside with moss; **(5)** place small plants forward; **(6)** tall plants in rear; **(7)** use glass cover; and **(8)** keep lid open if excess moisture gathers inside.

Gloxinias (above) can be grown from tubers. You'll learn how later in this chapter. Once a plant comes into bloom, keep it in light—not sun—and buds will unfold for weeks.

◄ A clivia that is grown as a house plant produces orange and yellow bloom in early spring. (For complete cultural information on this handsome amaryllis relative, see page 96.)

Favorite Flowering Plants

Everyone loves flowering house plants. Their blooms—sometimes fragrant, always colorful—catch and hold the eye. They make a unique addition to any decorating scheme.

Some house plants bloom for only brief seasons; others, almost continuously. Of the obliging beauties that put up bloom year-round, ever-flowering begonias and African violets head the list. Geraniums, close behind on the list of favorites, reward you with two seasons of bloom if you take stem cuttings at the proper time. Cuttings rooted in late summer bring fall and winter bloom in addition to spring and summer flowering.

Other flowering varieties are truly seasonal, to be enjoyed while their beauty lasts, then remembered and looked forward to for another year. Perhaps this enhances their desirability. Would amaryllis or tulips and hyacinths be as enchanting if you could have them in bloom every day?

The pages that follow contain information on how to grow all those mentioned and many more. Some are easy to grow, while others offer a challenge to indoor gardeners.

Use a sharp knife to sever leaf from mother plant **(1)** with one- to two-inch stem attached. Choose leaf with a firm, not a rubbery stem.

Dipping stem end **(2)** into a root-promoting powder is not essential, but it is an extra insurance of vigorous root formation.

Insert treated leaves in moistened vermiculite **(3)** or similar rooting mixture. Use small pot when rooting only a few leaves. Keep moist.

To start many leaves at once, use a cake pan **(4)** filled with rooting media that's uniformly moist. Use a plastic cover to trap moisture.

To root in water, cover jar with foil or wax paper **(5)**; punch holes in top; insert leaves. When roots are an inch long, pot in sandy soil.

Hundreds of new varieties of African violets have been developed in recent decades. This one (below), Blue Warrior, centers bloom.

African violets

A favorite house plant in millions of homes, the African violet isn't a violet at all, although it does come from Africa. *Saintpaulias,* to use the correct botanical name, keep on blooming for months on end and are among the easiest of all house plants to propagate. One good way to fill your home with different African violets is to join the African Violet Society, and you'll soon be trading leaves for propagation with collectors throughout the country to increase your treasury of varieties—violet, blue, white, and purple, plus soft pink—both single and double as well as ruffled.

HOW TO KEEP PLANTS GROWING AND BLOOMING

There are some tricks to growing profusely blooming African violets. Proper amount of light, water, and food are the big three.

An east or west window is usually best for African violets, as direct rays of south sun may burn the leaves. North windows, except during the summer, do not offer adequate light. You can also grow the plants under artificial light. (See pages 74-79.)

Watering can be done successfully with a wick-style container, since it keeps soil uniformly moist. Contrary to a widely held belief, it does the plant no harm to be watered from above, provided that the water is of room temperature—cold water spots leaves. Many experts on African violets feel that rainwater (or melted snow) is superior to tap water for these plants.

The best soil mixture is one-third each garden loam, coarse sand, and leaf mold or peat. The ideal room temperature range is from 70° to 75°. When house temperature drops below 60°, growth is slowed. For this reason, in very cold weather, plants in locations next to windows may need to be relocated or given night protection.

Feed established plants every other week, but don't fertilize newly potted or repotted plants for six to eight weeks. When you do fertilize the plants, use fertilizers that can be dissolved in water.

A frequent cause of nonflowering is a lack of humidity. A favorite location for growing African violets is in a kitchen window since cooking activities naturally produce higher humidity here than elsewhere.

You can also increase humidity by setting pots on a layer of pebbles in a tray. Keep water up to the level of the pebbles.

When new growth (top left), still attached to the mother leaf, is about this size, it's ready to shift to regular potting soil.

When plants are two or three inches tall (top right), you can separate rosettes, plant individually, or pot the whole clump in larger pot.

When potting (bottom), put piece of clay pot or a bottle cap over bottom hole to ensure drainage. Hold plant in center and fill.

Amaryllis for winter color

Monarch of the house plant world, nothing can rival the amaryllis for size of bloom and brilliance of color at a time when snow covers the ground and temperatures are well below freezing in most parts of the country.

You can buy amaryllis bulbs that have been 'cold-treated' so that they'll flower on schedule during the holidays. Choose a bulb that is large and has many live roots. Place it on top of a water-filled jar. This allows roots (not bulb) to trail in water. Let roots soak up extra moisture in this way four or five days before potting. For this step, follow pictures and text at right.

The length of time it takes for blooms to appear varies somewhat. As a general rule, you can expect to see fat buds begin to open in four to six weeks after potting.

Although the price of the choicest bulbs may seem high initially (name varieties of top quality cost in the neighborhood of five dollars), you are purchasing a plant that can—with proper care—go on blooming each winter for years to come. Pictures and text on the following pages show you how.

WARMTH, FOOD, AND WATER REQUIREMENTS

As natives of tropical climates, amaryllis like warmth and should be given a spot in your sunniest window until flowers begin to open. The bloom lasts longer if you then move the plant to medium light.

Because the plants grow so rapidly—you sometimes feel that you can actually see those big stems push upward—they need water often enough to keep the soil constantly moist. Once flower scapes appear, it's wise to begin giving the plant a weak feeding of fertilizer once a week, thus helping the bulb to begin forming next year's flower buds.

◄ Color range of big, hybrid bulbs is impressive. Buy clear red or white like these, or choose from pinks, corals, garnet reds, and also from striped, banded, or bordered varieties.

Size of bulb is important (top left). Bulb at right is too small. Buy those that are 2½ inches in diameter or larger. Bulb should have live roots and *may* show new growth at top.

First step (top right) is providing for drainage. Use pot (6-inch or larger) that's big enough to leave an inch of space around bulb. Half of bulb should remain above soil level.

Allow for watering (bottom left) by leaving an inch of space free at the top of pot. Water until excess drains out, using lukewarm water. Place the pot in a warm, sunny window.

Flower buds (bottom right) have a small indentation or dimple at the tip. If night temperatures in the window drop below 60°, move the plant to a warmer spot for the night.

As soon as blooms wither (top left), cut them off with a razor blade or knife so that no stub remains. When the stalks yellow, cut off where they emerge from bulb. Continue watering and feeding, keeping the plant in sunlight.

Help your bulb regain strength (top right) after blooming by giving it regular feedings. Use fertilizer in recommended amounts, either dry or in liquid form, according to the directions on the package given by the manufacturer.

When all danger of frost has passed, choose an outdoor location that receives some sun (bottom left). Dig a hole and place some gravel on the bottom for drainage. Then, sink the pot so that it is level with the soil.

Water and feed regularly during summer (bottom right). Lift before the first frost. Store dry in cool location for next two to three months. When the neck looks faintly green, bring to light and warmth and water regularly.

AFTERCARE IS IMPORTANT

What you do for your spring amaryllis after the bloom has faded and on through the following summer determines the fate of next year's flowering. Your care is undemanding so far as effort and time are concerned, but you must feed and water the plant on a faithful schedule. If you do, your bulb will build strength to form next year's buds.

At the end of summer (usually late September) and before freezing weather arrives, lift the pot, take it indoors, and store it in a cool location. Place the pot on its side, and water no further for the next few months. When the amaryllis is ready to begin its next growing cycle, the neck of the bulb will turn green. At that point, bring the pot to warmth and light and begin watering it regularly, adding some fresh potting soil at the top of the pot. The bulb will revert to normal blooming time—late winter.

In addition to the amaryllis, there are several related bulb plants, taking the same cultural attention, that also make interesting house plants. Among these are the tender crinum (hardy varieties are grown in the gardens in the South), sprekelia or 'orchid-lily,' brunsvigia, zephyranthes, sternbergia, and haemanthus or 'blood-lily.'

Not related (grown from tubers rather than bulbs), but good companions to amaryllis are those showy plants, the caladiums. Like the group pictured across the page, they can be obtained in many marbled leaf patterns that include reds, pinks, whites, and greens. Familiar as garden plants for shade, they're also excellent house plants.

Start caladium tubers in moist peat moss or sand. The roots grow from the tops of the tubers. After they start, repot (three tubers to a 7-inch pot) in a standard potting soil mixture, placing the tubers an inch below the soil. It takes six to eight weeks to reach the size pictured at the right.

The trumpet-shape of amaryllis blooms and the heart-shape of fancy-leaved caladium plants are mutually complementary. Both of these beautiful house plants come in a range of reds and whites to brighten winter indoors. ▶

Gloxinias in jewel tones

Success with growing gloxinias depends more on proper watering of the soil than on any other factor. Test the soil by squeezing some of it into a ball; if it falls apart when touched, it is too dry. Soil should be constantly moist, but not *wet*.

Gloxinias also require a warm, moist atmosphere during growth and blooming. Bright light, not direct sun, is needed, since tender foliage is subject to sunscald.

In general, the gloxinia requires much the same treatment as does the African violet: open, porous soil containing plenty of peat or leaf mold; strong light but not full sun; and watering with lukewarm water. It's also possible to reproduce gloxinias by the same method as African violets — by rooting leaves, as described on page 52.

Sinningia — botanical name of the gloxinia commonly grown by florists — also responds well to growing under light. Given 16 hours of light a day (about 8 inches below a pair of 40-watt tubes) and a humid atmosphere (50 percent), this plant is easy to maintain in this growing situation. Your tuber should bloom within three to four months. (See section on growing plants under artificial lights for more information.)

WHAT TO LOOK FOR
IN A TUBER

The size of a tuber (they vary from 1 to 3 inches in diameter) is less important than its quality. It should feel firm to the touch — neither dry nor soft. If soft, the bulb is usually rotten. Larger tubers should be potted singly; smaller tubers, two or three to a pot. In either case use a 5- or 6-inch pot of shallow type called a 'bulb pan,' since plant at maturity is low and spreads.

◀ After gloxinias flower, reduce amount of water given daily until the soil is almost dry. Store pot in a cool place (not over 60°) with low light. Check often; water occasionally. When leaves emerge, repot, and bring to the light.

Healthy tubers (top) should feel firm, have pinkish new growth on topside, have roots below, and show dry bits of last year's growth.

Provide for bottom drainage (middle). Then, fill lower half of pot with soil. Hold tuber in one hand while sifting soil about the roots.

Tubers started in vermiculite or other growing medium (bottom) may be shifted to regular pots and potting soil when growth looks like this.

Scarlet bloom and colorful foliage of Happy Thought (1) make it a favorite among large group of fancy-leaf geraniums. Single flowers.

Distinction (2) has small-toothed, round, green leaves with distinct circle markings near outer edge of each leaf. Single flowers.

Cherry Sundae (3) bears many double, cherry-red flowers, has attractive silvery green leaves, that are edged and blotched with white.

1

2

3

4
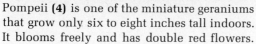
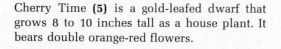

5

Pompeii (4) is one of the miniature geraniums that grow only six to eight inches tall indoors. It blooms freely and has double red flowers.

6

Cherry Time (5) is a gold-leafed dwarf that grows 8 to 10 inches tall as a house plant. It bears double orange-red flowers.

Springfield violet (6) is a dark, nearly purple, zonal geranium, handsome outdoors. Make fall cuttings for indoor winter bloom.

Geraniums that bloom in all seasons

It's easy to see why the geranium is such a popular flowering plant. Big heads of bloom look like gay, little umbrellas and their foliage has a spicy scent. They bloom indoors during winter months, and can be moved out to the porch, patio, or garden in summer.

Varieties of this old-fashioned favorite have been vastly expanded in recent years—the group pictured across the page is only a small sampling of the hybridizers' artistry in developing colorful foliage and miniature and dwarf varieties with novel hues.

Undemanding in most matters, geraniums won't tolerate shade. They need sun each day, or they grow 'leggy' and refuse to bloom. Give them a spot in a sunny window, and pinch back tall stems after blooming.

Temperatures ranging from 60° to 70° are ideal, and plenty of fresh air and high humidity help to ensure good performance.

Potted geraniums do best when allowed to become quite dry between waterings. Water thoroughly—until the water runs out of the bottom drainage hole. Empty the saucer and don't water again until the soil is dry.

MAKE CUTTINGS FOR WINTER BLOOM

If you grow geraniums outdoors in summer and want them to bloom again in winter or in early spring, you must take cuttings from the parent plant before fall dormancy sets in—early August in most sections. Pictures and text below show you how to do it.

Take 3- to 5-inch cuttings (top left), making a cut just below leaf node. Avoid soft, immature or old, branches. Cut away bottom leaves.

Root cuttings (after dipping in root-promoting powder, if desired) (top right) in moist vermiculite or other growing medium.

Cuttings are ready to pot in potting soil when roots are 1½ to 2 inches long—in four to six weeks. Use a 4-inch pot and supply drainage.

When you buy lily of the valley pips prepared for forcing (top left), there's little you need to do, except to give them a sunny window and check water needs daily to keep growing medium moist, *not* wet. Blooms in three weeks.

Paper-white narcissus (top right) and a near relative, Soleil d'Or (rich, golden yellow in bloom), are tender bulbs that need no period of cold before starting to grow indoors. Follow directions given in text on opposite page.

You can depend on King Alfred daffodils (bottom) to force easily. Crocus is less certain. Bring pots of crocus to a cool, bright window as soon as you lift the pots from the trench. After a week, move to a sunny window.

Forced bulbs for indoor bloom

By a process known as 'forcing,' which means to bring to bloom at earlier than normal date, you can coax a host of spring stars to flower indoors weeks and even months before you could have them in the garden. Tulips, hyacinths, daffodils, and crocus all need a prolonged cold period before they can be forced. Except for a commercial handler who uses refrigeration, this requires garden space. Even apartment dwellers can force other bulb plants to bloom indoors.

Earliest of all is the paper-white narcissus, pictured on the facing page. Bulbs are on the market early each fall, and you can have your first bowlful of fragrant bloom in time for Thanksgiving, if you like.

All you need do is to set the bulbs in a bowl of pebbles or marble chips to supply stability. Keep the bowl filled with water to height of pebbles, and place it in a sunny window. Blooms will follow shortly.

Lily of the valley (*Convallaria majalis*) can be purchased as cold-treated pips. They are usually sold already packed in a moist, fibrous growing medium. Slip the ready-to-grow package into an attractive container, set it in a sunny window, water often enough to keep the fiber moist, and expect fragrant bloom in about three weeks.

STARTING BULBS IN OUTDOOR BEDS

If you have garden space, you'll want to experiment with tulips, hyacinths, daffodils, and the many smaller spring-flowering bulbs that lend themselves to forcing. In general, the larger the bulb, the simpler it is to force. You can advance the chances of success by asking for early varieties. The later a bulb blooms outdoors, the harder it will be to force it later on.

The process of forcing involves duplicating —but shortening—the normal stages the bulbs pass through in the garden: **(1)** fall planting (in bulb pans sunk outdoors); **(2)** a prolonged period of cold weather (this period is reduced to about 12 weeks in forcing); and **(3)** warmth and sunshine to make buds open.

Partially fill bulb pans (shallower than standard pots) with potting soil. Set bulbs into pots so that noses are just below pot rim. Don't overcrowd. Firm soil with fingers or by thumping pot to settle. Water bulbs thoroughly.

Prepare trench twice the depth of pots, and line it with hay, dry leaves, or evergreen clippings. Set pots in trench so that rims are 2 inches below soil level. Stakes and labels identify pots. Fill around and over pots with soil.

When shoots are 1 to 3 inches tall and pot is filled with roots (tap one out to check), bring pots indoors. Keep dark and at a cool temperature (60°) for a week, watering frequently. Then, bring pots into a warm, sunny window.

An ample water supply from the time you pot and sink bulbs on through the fall until the ground freezes is vital to success in forcing, to promote rapid root growth.

In warm areas, delay potting and sinking the bulbs until cold weather comes—nights in the forties. Soil temperatures should be below 48°, but the bulbs should not freeze.

Allow at least 12 weeks of cold weather to pass before you lift the pots and bring them indoors to 60° basement temperatures. Continue to water as needed after you bring the pots in.

When you're ready to lift the pots, take up one, check both top growth (3-inch shoots) and root growth. Tap out one pot and check the roots to be certain they largely fill the bottom soil.

Normally, from the time you plant the spring-flowering bulbs until they bloom, a period of from seven to eight months elapses. By forcing, you can cut that time in half.

Select a site for your outdoor trench (as shown in the sketch on page 63) where sun reaches it, softens soil, and makes it easy for you to lift pots when the proper time arrives. South locations are best for this reason. If you have a cold frame, it, too, can be used successfully for forcing bulbs. In either case, water the sunken pots of bulbs through the fall until the ground freezes.

Lifting pots without breaking them is easier if you line the trench with dry vegetation— even excelsior—before setting the pots into place. Then, after setting the pots in place, put down a top protective layer of dry vegetation before filling trench with soil. Finally, mound leaves over the trench for added protection. Ensure that the leaves do not blow away by laying a board on top of them.

After at least 12 weeks of cold weather (see drawings and text above), lift a pot to see if the roots fill the soil ball and if the shoots are up by at least three inches. If so, bring the bulbs indoors.

Move the pots first to the basement (or a location where the temperature isn't above 60°) for one week. Continue to water the plant as needed, but make sure it doesn't receive any light by covering the pots with paper bags. Then, bring the pots to a sunny window. As the buds swell and the flowers open, continue to water the plant.

For success in forcing tulips, it's important to choose the right varieties. Among those recommended for early forcing (brought indoors after mid-January) are: Brilliant Star, Cassini, De Wet (reds), Bellona (yellow), and Pink Perfection. Tulips that are good for later forcing (after February 1) are: Her Grace (white edged in pink), Merry Widow (red bordered with white), and Orange Wonder. Your bulb dealer may recommend others.

Once in bloom, keep the plants out of sunlight ▶ for longer life. When blooms fade, move the daffodils or hyacinths to a cool window; continue to water. When ground softens, plant in the garden for next year's bloom. It's not worth the effort for tulips that have been forced.

Longer lives for gift plants

Delight over a blooming plant can turn to keen disappointment if you don't know how to give it proper care. You can feel quite resentful—unjustifiably so—if you mistakenly assume that all plants should live on indefinitely, as do many foliage plants.

It is best to simply face the fact that some of the seasonal flowering plants are to be looked upon as if they were cut flowers—to be enjoyed while they last and to be discarded when they fade.

A number of those traditionally given or received as gifts cannot bloom or live long except under greenhouse conditions—so different from the desertlike atmosphere that characterizes most homes in winter.

With a few exceptions (to be mentioned in later paragraphs) seasonal blooming plants will last longest in your home if you give them a cool, light (not sunny) location and ample water of room temperature. It takes a lot of water to produce and sustain bloom, and water requirements should be checked on each day so that the plant doesn't wilt. If you've slipped your gift plant into a watertight container, you must also check on drainage, for if the pot stands in water, the roots will almost always rot. Blasts or drafts of either hot or cold air, too, reduce the life of your gift plants, so try to choose a location that promotes healthy growth.

TIPS ON SPECIFIC PLANT NEEDS

Cyclamen is an example of a plant commonly received as a gift in winter months that *needs* sun in order to continue blooming. Although it may have only five or six blooms showing when you receive it, a good specimen has dozens of buds at the crown. These will all push up and bloom if you provide a cool,

Container-grown holly (upper left), poinsettia (upper right), cyclamen (center), and Christmas begonia take special care to keep in good condition. (For details, see text at right.)

sunny window and ample water. Pour water in at the pot's edge—not into crown. Provide adequate drainage for the plant.

Poinsettias, too, need bright light in order to hold their color, and adequate humidity to prevent bottom leaf drop. In a cool but sunny window, with daily watering and good drainage, and with a room humidity upwards of 30 percent, a Christmas poinsettia may still be attractive at Easter.

If you want to carry this plant over for another year, sink the pot in a sunny garden location after frost danger has passed. Prune the stems severely, and water and fertilize regularly until the cool nights arrive. Then, lift the pot and bring it indoors again to a cool, sunny window, and you *might* receive the bonus of another season of bloom.

Azaleas of varieties sold as florists' pot plants may not be hardy in your climate. If they are, however, they can be planted outdoors in a suitable, partly shaded location as early in spring as possible, given the same care you would give any newly set shrub, with regular watering the first year. If not hardy in your region, the same aftercare described for poinsettias, though with mild pruning, may bring you successive seasons of bloom, probably somewhat sparse.

Christmas begonia is the only one of the gift plants pictured opposite (bottom right) incapable of long life under home conditions. Lush growth comes from energy stored while growing in a greenhouse. Enjoy the color while you can. When it's through, it's through and must be discarded.

Holly bushes, container grown, if hardy in your climate, can be set outdoors as early in the spring as possible. Give them partial shade, and water them frequently.

If the evergreen hollies are not hardy in your region, you may wish to keep yours as a pot plant. If so, supply a cool, sunny location, ample water, and high humidity.

Bulb plants (hyacinths, daffodils, and crocus), if given proper aftercare, can be set out in appropriate garden locations for future years of bloom. (See also page 65.)

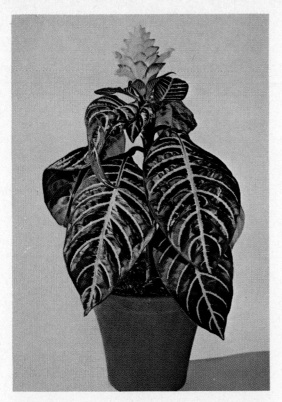

Aphelandra is one of the many exotic plants widely sold by florists today. It requires green-house humidity to flourish and bloom. (See page 101 for additional information.)

◀ Full instructions came with this packaged lean-to greenhouse, so the homeowner installed it himself in the frame of a former picture window. (See page 70 for an outside view.)

Greenhouses and Gardens Under Lights

In recent years, there have been a number of exciting developments to interest all who delight in the presence of plants in their homes: mass production (and lower cost) of small greenhouses; production of inexpensive equipment for growing plants under lights; and increasing numbers of homes designed in atrium style (a garden in a central, enclosed position, as was common in Roman houses), or with a small viewing garden extending from almost any room in the home.

Along with these innovations has come the greatly expanded availability of exotics — such plants as orchids, bromeliads, and Japanese bonsai — and information concerning how to grow them. Together, these developments have made it entirely feasible for today's amateur to grow plants once considered only within the range of highly trained horticulturists working in conservatories.

In the pages of this chapter, you are invited to sample the excitement of all of these possibilities. Select an idea that particularly appeals to you, and greatly increase the daily joy of indoor gardening.

This 11x13 greenhouse (above) was ordered as a kit and assembled according to instructions. It makes an ideal transition from a family room to the garden and outdoor living area. The deck and steps lead to back entrance.

This lean-to greenhouse, which is pictured from the inside on page 68, shows how old bricks were used for the foundation to harmonize with the house. Tree branches protect against too strong a sun during the summer.

Good design suits this plant room to the house of which it is an extension. In outside view (above), notice that the roof is of chicken-wire glass—strong enough to support weight of possible snow. Inside (below), the U-shaped bench brings all plants within easy reach. Gravel-lined metal trays allow for convenience in watering and good drainage afterward.

CHOOSING A GREENHOUSE

Because the range of choices is so wide, including prefab and custom-built styles, it is impossible to tell you what greenhouse you should have. A good way to begin exploring the possibilities, though, is to secure free literature from the many firms who manufacture styles including freestanding, lean-to, and window greenhouses. This will give you an idea of what is available and the price range—two important factors.

Once you know the basic cost, add the expenses of installing or extending existing heat and water lines to the structure. Also, where winters are severe, the cost of building a masonry foundation that goes well below the frostline must be added.

Before you proceed with the installation, check on local building and zoning codes to make sure that your plan is in accordance with existing regulations.

Location is another important factor. A greenhouse should receive southerly light if it is to support a wide variety of flowering plants. Morning sun is important; late afternoon sun counts for little.

Heat and ventilation are also essential. You may be able to attach a greenhouse outlet to equipment you now have. However, you can buy a heater built for the purpose.

The size of your greenhouse is important, too. Don't build too small a house. It's hard to ventilate and heat small areas under glass; temperature zooms when the sun comes up; drops almost as fast when it goes down.

Lastly, ample ventilation by sashes in the roof and ends is needed. A large opening into the house (for lean-to styles) is a help. It cuts down heat-absorbing wall space and offers an extra volume of air to cushion against rapid temperature changes.

The most satisfactory way to ventilate any type of greenhouse is by means of thermostatic control. A thermostat automatically opens and shuts if temperature rises above or falls below the degree of desired heat.

If the conventional styles of greenhouses are too expensive for you, consider converting a porch or garage to your needs. In either case, corrugated plastic roofing and heavy plastic sheeting in place of glass may bring a greenhouse within your reach.

The atrium garden

Although making architectural news today, the atrium house dates back to the Romans, who found a retreat from hot summers in the central courtyard of their homes — the atrium.

Today's atrium house differs greatly in many ways from its Roman antecedents. But, like those ancient dwellings, it offers a private garden world to those who dwell in crowded urban and suburban centers.

In all but very warm climates, the modern atrium is ordinarily roofed and lighted by skylights, clerestory windows, or a plastic bubble. Each of these can provide for ventilation during warm weather, with vents that can be opened when necessary.

The atrium need not be placed at the exact center of the house. However, it should be positioned so that the main living rooms can share in the delights of a garden that winter cannot touch — a constantly green vista in all the months of the year.

PLANTS SUITED TO THE ATRIUM

More than in other forms of indoor gardens, plantings of an atrium should be chosen with due consideration for local climate. In warm regions, you can grow almost anything in an atrium that will grow outdoors. On the other hand, in colder growing zones, the atrium would, in all likelihood, be operated as a cool greenhouse (night temperature in the 50s, day temperatures in the 60s), thus ruling out heat lovers such as the amaryllis, and slowing down growth of house plants preferring warmer house temperatures.

But choices are still vast. Such broadleaf evergreens as camellias, azaleas, and gardenias make excellent choices, and all can be kept to desirable heights with pruning. Grass is not a good choice for ground cover,

since it requires mowing. But periwinkle, pachysandra, ajuga, dichondra, ivy, and many others make a green carpet that takes little attention other than watering.

A good-looking, minimum-care, atrium garden is easy to grow if the gardener relies on smaller shrubs and trees (not deciduous varieties, which require a period of cold and dormancy), ground cover, and foliage plants. As with outdoor gardens, it is easy to have splashes of seasonal color with container-grown flowering plants that are easy to lift and replace when period of bloom has ended.

Simplify watering chores a great deal by adding a water outlet to which a garden hose can be connected. An atrium garden also needs floor drains for excess water. A path of brick, flagstone, or gravel offers easy access to all of the planted areas.

Floor plan shows how the living room, kitchen, and family room are separated only by the central placement of an atrium garden. Entrances bracket the garden, so all routes in and out of the house share the view of the plantings.

◀ Kitchen (behind brick wall) and garden share daylight from skylight of slightly gray plexiglass at roof's peak. The garden is a 16-inch depression in the concrete floor of the house.

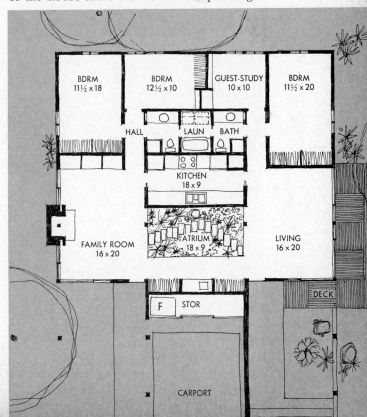

Little gardens on wheels are available in several sizes, equipped with light tubes and waterproof plant trays. Plug them in wherever you like. The only disadvantage is that they permit little adjustment in height of lights.

Build benches into a basement corner if you're interested in extensive gardening under lights. Each bench should be equipped with a waterproof tray to take care of drainage. This is an ideal arrangement for growing seedlings.

Among the smaller light units commercially available is this simple, but attractive model designed for tabletop placement. Here, it's

used to display pots of kalanchoe that have reached the blooming stage. Light height is adjusted by knobs at sides of framework.

Gardening under lights

You can grow luxuriant house plants in any spot in your home with the aid of man-made sunshine—electric light. Corners so dark that they'd discourage even a cast-iron plant are turned into garden spots by using the right amount of artificial light.

Most house plants get too little light in winter months, not only because of the low light intensity characteristic of that period of the year, but also because of the shortness of daylight hours. To remedy this, the perfect winter situation for most house plants is in daylight by day, with a boost from artificial light during both daytime and part of the hours after dark.

There are many plants that can thrive for varying periods of time on nothing but artificial light—in amounts an average gardener can supply at moderate cost. African violets, begonias, and gloxinias are examples of the blooming varieties that perform well without ever catching a glimpse of the sun.

WHERE TO LOCATE
A LIGHT SETUP

Enthusiasts for gardening under artificial light have placed their setups all over the house—from living rooms to basements, even in closets! If you intend to grow large numbers of plants and to experiment with propagation from seeds and cuttings, the basement is best. It offers ample space and a lower temperature than the rooms in which you live—probably 55 to 65 degrees—which is better for most house plants. When the plants are in bloom, transfer them to the rooms you occupy.

You can start on as small a scale as you wish—one plant under a table lamp. If you use an incandescent bulb, it should be of at least 75-watt size and placed no more than four feet above the foliage, but no closer than two feet. Fluorescent tubes, because they burn cooler, can be placed as close as 6 to 8 inches from plants.

There are many possible variations that work well and are decorative, too. Try a light cart such as the one pictured in the upper left-hand corner of the facing page, or an attractive tabletop unit like the one below it. If a handyman is willing to design and build them to fit a special space in your home, you can have handsome wall units like those pictured on the following pages.

You may use either incandescent or fluorescent lights for this kind of gardening, but experiments have shown that a combination of fluorescent and incandescent light is better than either used alone. Generally, it is beneficial to supplement with some incandescent light, particularly when a 'daylight' fluorescent tube is used.

Research studies indicate that a plant will live and stay attractive for at least a year if it is lighted for 16 hours daily with the minimum light intensity it needs. (Lists on page 79 group plants according to their minimum light requirements in terms of footcandles per day.) If you intend to grow plants in large quantities, you may want to obtain a light meter to test footcandles available in your light setup, checking on amounts obtainable at differing numbers of inches below light. (For most of the flowering plants, from 8 to 10 inches below light tubes is best.)

Most beginners find that using two 48-inch, 40-watt tubes of the type specifically made for growing plants (including both blue and red rays) offer flexibility—good growing conditions for a variety of plants.

Commercial fixtures are available inexpensively. However, you can construct your own. If you do, provide a reflector that is painted white or foil-lined to direct the light downward onto plants. Notice that in the basement setup pictured across the page the walls and ceiling have been painted white, thereby gaining maximum benefit from reflection of artificial light onto plants.

If you use a light meter to check on available footcandles, you will notice that the light is strongest at the center, and weakest at the ends of tubes. You can take advantage of this by placing those plants needing the most light in a central position, flanking them at ends with plants requiring less.

Combination bookcase-house plant center takes just three feet of wall space. Above the plants, a false drawer neatly conceals the fluorescent light fixture. A metal tray in the recessed top of the base cabinet simplifies watering.

Indoor gardeners who'd like to experiment with growing plants under lights on a small scale will find the units pictured here of great interest. Either one can be built by a handyman with limited carpentry skills. Both include some convenient storage space for supplies. And both, since they are built as pieces of furniture, can be installed in any room of your house or apartment, taking up a minimum of floor space.

If you decide to build your light setup — whether large or small — you should begin by knowing the standard sizes in which tube lamps are made: 15-inch (14-watt); 18-inch (15-watt); 24-inch (20-watt); 33-inch (25-watt); 36-inch (30-watt); 48-inch (40-watt); and 96-inch (72-watt). Fixtures for each size, including the sockets for the tubes, are slightly longer than the tube length.

If you use two 48-inch tubes of 40-watts each, side by side and spaced 6 inches apart, you will have a growing area of about 4 square feet (48 x 12 inches), and can obtain from 15 to 20 watts of light per square foot for plants grown below them — the standard amount plants must have for healthy growth. It is always advisable to mount the tubes side by side rather than end to end in order to get maximum growing area in relation to lamp wattage. But unless you can get to a light setup from both sides, more than two side by side are impractical since you would have difficulty reaching across front plants to get at those in the rear.

Lamps should be installed so that they are not more than 15 inches above the tops of plants; 8 inches is considered ideal. You may choose from daylight or natural fluorescents as well as from among several varieties of tube lights designed for indoor gardens. Some veteran light gardeners find using one fluorescent and one plant tube in each fixture gives better results than either type used alone. But this is something you should experiment with for yourself, since little has been definitively established on this subject, and results vary widely depending upon the varieties of plants that are grown under lights.

Although length of life for tube lights is somewhat variable, you should probably plan to replace yours after about a year of use if they have been operated on a 16-hour basis for that period. Often you'll be able to see that the lamp has darkened, but even if you cannot, it's probably not producing the original amount of wattage.

PLANTS NEED BOTH LIGHT AND DARKNESS

The effect of daylight hours on blooming plants has long been recognized by scientists who have done research on plant growth habits. It's known that some plants are triggered to bloom by short days (chrysanthemums, for example); others — including most all of the garden annuals — by longer days. A third group, and most house plants are in this one, seem to be unaffected by day length. But it is a well-known fact that *all* plants need a period of darkness in each 24-hour period. For this reason, it is important to establish a regular schedule for turning the lights on and off in your garden under lights.

To help you do this accurately, an automatic timer (they cost about $10), which you can set to turn lights on and off at the times you choose, is an item that is well worth the money. Most flowering plants need about 16 hours of artificial light, while foliage plants do well on 10 or 12 hours. If you grow a mixture of plants, set the timer for the number of hours needed by the flowering varieties, since a few extra hours will do no harm to the foliage plants.

OTHER PLANT NEEDS

In addition to light and darkness, plants need more humidity than is available in an average home in winter months. For sizeable light gardens, such as the basement unit pictured on page 74, it is worthwhile to install a small fan to keep the air circulating (though not blowing directly onto plants) and one of the cool vapor-type humidifiers, which are capable of putting out from 2 to 10 gallons of water in a 24-hour period.

For small light gardens, humidity can be increased by lining waterproof plant trays with pebbles, sand, vermiculite, or peat moss and by keeping the material moist. Care must be taken that pots don't stand in water. Excess water will cause root rot for some varieties. Heavy plastic hung over sides of shelves, ends open for circulation, is also effective in raising humidity, but is not attractive if your light garden is located in the lived-in areas of your home.

Still another way to increase humidity is by frequent misting, using water of room temperature. Handy syringe bottles for this purpose are on the market at low cost. Avoid misting after noon, for plants shouldn't have wet foliage when lights go off.

When feeding plants-under-lights, you can use the same liquid fertilizer that you use for other house plants, diluted in the same proportion and applied at intervals suggested by the manufacturer. Or, since watering is less frequent due to higher humidity, you may wish to do as some experts recommend: feed plants at about one-fourth strength whenever you water them.

Two-tier planter provides artificial light for plants on lower shelf; those above get sun at the window ledge. Metal plant trays filled with pebbles let you increase humidity in the immediate vicinity of the plants.

Remodeling an older home or building a new one can include plans for a tropical view garden. Sliding glass doors make it easy to maintain desired humidity and ceiling light panels supply light for selected foliage plants.

An entrance planting that lacks natural light can be grown attractively by installing recessed ceiling spotlights. Rubber plant, monstera, dracaena, and dieffenbachia are suitable choices for a low light situation like this.

If your garden-under-light is an architectural or decorative feature such as those pictured on the facing page, you can, by choosing foliage plants that tolerate low light, make use of ceiling-level lighting. You can choose from circle-line tubes, panel lighting, and fluorescent as well as incandescent lights mounted in fixtures that are designed to cast light onto plants without producing unpleasant glare in a room.

Excessive heat builds up if large numbers of incandescent bulbs are grouped together in a small area. Through an electrical supply company, you can order 130-volt bulbs, which will be somewhat cooler.

Although very few plants 'thrive' under conditions of low artificial light, there are a number of plants that remain attractive for long periods of time. You will do well to make use of the following lists for help in selecting these as well as plants that will flourish under normal light-garden wattage.

Plants for low artificial light
Acorus gramineus
Aglaonema (Chinese Evergreen)
Asparagus fern
Asparagus sprengeri
Bertolonia
Chlorophytum
Cissus (Grape Ivy)
Cyperus alternifolius (Umbrella Plant)
Dieffenbachia amoena
Dieffenbachia picta
Dizygotheca
Dracaena (most varieties)
Ficus (Rubber Plant)
Nephrolepis
Nephthytis
Palms (most varieties)
Philodendron cordatum
Philodendron panduriforme
Philodendron pertusum
Pittosporum
Podocarpus
Pteris (table ferns)
Sansevieria species
Schefflera
Scindapsus
Tolmiea menziesii (Pickaback Plant)
Tradescantia (most varieties)

Foliage plants recommended for average light-garden conditions
Adiantum (Maidenhair Fern)
Aloe species
Alternanthera (Joseph's Coat)
Anthurium Scherzerianum
Aphelandra
Araucaria (Norfolk Island Pine)
Asplenium nidus (Bird's-nest Fern)
Aucuba
Begonia species
Caladium
Cissus anctarctica (Kangaroo Vine)
Coleus
Croton
Cyrtomium falcatum (Holly Fern)
Dracaena godseffiana (Gold Dust Dracaena)
Fatshedera
Fittonia
Hedera helix (English Ivy)
Maranta (Prayer Plant)
Peperomia species
Pilea cadierei (Aluminum Plant)
Platycerium alcicorne (Staghorn Fern)
Rhoeo spathacea (Three Men in a Boat)

Flowering plants for average light-garden conditions
Abutilon (Flowering Maple)
Achimenes
Agapanthus (Lily of the Nile)
Anthurium
Azalea
Bromeliads
Camellia japonica
Cineraria
Cyclamen
Episcia
Exacum
Gardenia
Gloxinia (Sinningia species)
Hibiscus
Hoya
Impatiens
Kalanchoe
Orchids (Cypripediums and Phalaenopsis varieties)
Oxalis
Pelargonium species (Geraniums)
Saintpaulia species (African Violets)
Streptocarpus (Cape Primrose)
Tuberous Begonias

Sample the exotics

Many unusual plants are cultivated indoors, but those under discussion here—orchids, bromeliads, and the bonsai method of dwarfing—deserve special mention.

orchids

Success with orchids need not depend upon special equipment and complicated know-how. Many indoor gardeners have proven this by flowering them in sunny windows. Start with a plant or two of blooming size, and you'll have the reward of flowers while you're learning how to care for your plants.

Grow your first orchids indoors near an east or south window—they need brightest light possible, but no direct sunlight in the warmer months. Foliage will give you a clue to light needs: pale foliage indicates too much light; dark green, the opposite.

Humidity is a must. Provide it by setting the plants on pebbles in a tray of water. Keep the water level below the top of the pebbles, as the roots of most orchid varieties will rot if constantly moist. It is helpful to mist-spray plants regularly, though this should be done in the morning, for plants should dry off before dark. Or buy a small cool vapor humidifier for the room.

Circulation of air is another vital need of orchids, so growing them at a window in a main room of the house offers advantages in this respect. Avoid direct drafts, however.

With a modest collection of fewer than a dozen plants, it is possible to have some in bloom all year long, since different varieties bloom at different seasons. Orchids flower once on a pseudobulb, so next year's bloom will be on new growths made this year.

◀ When an orchid is mentioned, most people think of a cattleya (left). These come in a variety of color combinations and bloom impressively from late spring on through summer months.

Cymbidium orchids (top picture) put forth spikes with up to 30 lovely flowers each in late fall and winter. Almost every hue, including bronze and green, is found in the group.

Cypripedium flowers will stay fresh for six to eight weeks on the plants or three weeks in a corsage. It is one of the easiest orchids to grow under lights. (See pages 78-79.)

bromeliads

A delightfully bizarre group of plants, the bromeliads have long starred in botanical garden exhibits, attracting attention with their brilliant blooms and their neat rosettes of foliage—often so shiny that they appear to have been varnished.

Many can be classed as succulents because they often store an emergency supply of water; not inside fleshy leaves as true succulents do, but in a natural, vase-shaped center formed by their durable foliage.

Natives of the tropical forests of Central and South America, bromeliads fall into two distinct groups: terrestrials, which grow in soil or between rocks; and epiphytes, which are (like some orchid varieties) tree dwellers. Many of the plants in the second group can exist for long periods of time without roots, as long as they receive moisture from reservoirs in their leaf bases.

Despite their exotic appearance and curious growth habits, bromeliads are considered to be exceptionally easy to grow.

When you buy one of these ornamental members of the pineapple family (see portfolio section for an example of fruiting variety), you may think it needs repotting. Not so. Root systems are limited and need little space, so the pot is always small and seemingly out of proportion to the size of the plant. Actually, roots are short holdfasts, which permit these plants in their natural state to cling to tree branches.

Roots are accustomed to free air circulation, so give them good drainage. When you buy a plant, it may have been potted in osmunda or shredded tree fern bark. If you don't have either material on hand when it's time to repot offsets (discussed later), you can use a soil mixture that's from one-third to one-half perlite or coarse sand. Using a porous potting mixture provides the open drainage that is essential to the health of this family of plants—waterlogged soil would mean certain death to the roots. But happily, there's no guesswork in watering bromeliads. Roots require little moisture—a soaking once a week will do. The main thing is to keep water in the center of the plant where you can see it at all times. When the water evaporates, replenish.

Resist the temptation that some amateurs succumb to of placing cut blooms from another plant inside the water cup of a bromeliad at times when it is not in bloom. A stiff stem inserted there can easily pierce and damage the heart of the bromeliad, ruining a flower bud that is forming inside.

Feeding bromeliads is optional. Some bromeliad hobbyists report of plants in their collections that have grown for years, content with whatever nutriments that they receive from the water. But if you belong to the school of indoor gardeners that believes strongly in fertilizing, a small amount of liquid fish emulsion (diluted according to package directions and used half strength) in the central water cup of the plant should be of some benefit if applied every six to eight weeks during the summer months.

Freedom from insect troubles is a major asset of bromeliads as house plants. But if scale (hard-bodied brown specks on leaves) should attack one of your plants, remove it from the leaf with your fingernail or wash it off with soap and water. Chances are slim that your plant will ever encounter scale, but if it does, take immediate action; neglect will only aggravate the problem.

Leaf burning—the result of putting plants in full sun for extended periods—is almost the only other bromeliad problem. This rarely occurs, however, for none of the bromeliads needs full sun. In fact, the soft-, green-leaved types, such as some of the vriesias, *must* be grown in shade. Those with stiff foliage, such as many neoregelias, do need very bright light, but you needn't line these plants up by a sunny window where you have to regulate light intensity during the day by shades or draperies. They will thrive as well six feet away from an outdoor light source. When in bloom, you can place them anywhere.

◀ *Vriesia fenestralis* (far left) has distinctive, broad foliage decorated with a network of fine, dark lines. *Nidularium innocentii lineatum,* (upper right) shows stripes of ivory on lettuce-green leaves. At bottom, another vriesia.

These eight plants give you an idea of the variations you will find in bromeliads—both in flower form and in foliage. Grown as house plants, the majority will begin to bloom in late winter, carrying on through spring.

Like many other house plants, bromeliads benefit from being moved outdoors in summer, where natural humidity is high and air can circulate freely around them. But be sure to choose a spot where they will receive only filtered light, never full summer sun.

HOW TO GROW MORE BROMELIADS

Bromeliads increase by making offsets, in much the same manner as do the familiar garden iris and daylily. However, the bromeliad differs from these plants in that it flowers only once, then dies gradually.

It is the offspring that carry on in successive years with bloom. So don't, generously, give away all your offsets, or you'll be left with a has-been bromeliad.

As the parent plant dies, the leaves turn brown. Simply peel them off as they loosen and become unsightly. Offsets grow against

The chart below gives botanical names of varieties shown at left. Few have common names. Aechmea group produces good offsets.

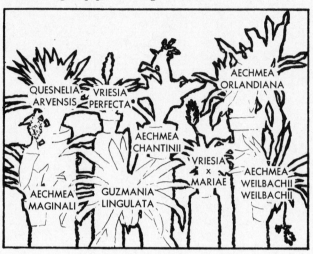

What to do with house plants when you're away? It's no problem if you grow bromeliads. Simply fill centers with water. Whether they're aechmeas (left) or vriesias (right), they won't miss your care at all for two or three weeks.

Neoregilia spectabilis, a popular bromeliad, has metallic-green leaves that end in pronounced tips of contrasting blood red. This accounts for its common name, painted fingernail plant. Blooms are fiery-red bells.

The most porous potting media are osmunda and shredded tree fern bark—the same you'd use for orchids. But soil with a liberal admixture of perlite or coarse sand will make a satisfactory substitute.

Barely cover the base of the new plant. Fasten the plant to a stake so that it will stay upright until it has had time to develop a root system for its own support.

If you have a large collection of bromeliads including several varieties, you'll be able to have some of the plants in bloom almost every month of the year.

Once the bromeliads are in bloom, the brilliantly colorful bracts, which most people think of as flowers are amazingly long-lasting. Some of them retain their attractive color for as long as six months—an undisputed record that no other flowering house plant can ever hope to equal!

Once it's in bloom, this modern-looking bromeliad, *Guzmania lingulata*, can be used to decorate the center of your dining room table. Even in dim light, it will thrive for weeks. Once bloom goes, return the plant to brighter light.

or close to the parent plant. Some kinds really proliferate, such as some of the aechmeas; others multiply less freely, such as *Vriesia splendens* (flaming sword), and produce only one or occasionally two new plants, which appear from the center cup of the old plant.

Suckers or offsets should be at least 4 inches tall before you detach them from the parent plant for individual potting. Gently remove fiber or soil so that you can see the entire root system clearly. The offset should have roots or show roots starting (indicated by slight bulges around the firm base of the plant). If there is space to cut, it's safe to use pruning shears; if plant and plantlet practically touch, use a sharp knife when you sever them.

Center the new plant in a 4-inch pot. This size will hold the parent plant and its future offshoots for three years, unless you prefer only single-plant specimens.

bonsai

Man's universal fascination with miniatures is nowhere more clearly seen than in his appreciation of those small, living works of art called bonsai. Translated, the Japanese name for these cultural dwarfs means tray trees. Their inspiration lies in nature itself— in gnarled, twisted trees of appealing form, seen on rocky cliffs, that survive despite poor soil and little water.

Widespread interest in bonsai followed American occupation of Japan at the close of World War II. Today, it is possible to buy mature specimens in many parts of the country, and more and more enthusiasts are learning the basics of training and care.

To the uninitiated, it should at once be made clear that bonsai are not primarily house plants, although they can be brought indoors several times a week to be seen at close range and enjoyed for perfection of form or for colorful seasonal bloom.

Well-grown bonsai must spend a major portion of their lives outdoors, in a situation similar to that pictured at the top of the following page, or in a cool greenhouse. They need the kind of light and humidity (some require cold, dormant periods) that cannot be duplicated in average homes. In climates with cold winters and hot summers, they need protection from extremes.

To create an artistic bonsai, the Japanese start with a young plant that, preferably, is already somewhat stunted or misshapen. Then, they prune both roots and branches regularly over many years. At the same time, they wrap the trunk and branches in wire to train them into pleasing lines. The wires remain in place for several years.

The pictures and the text at right supply you with information on how to start training a young plant as a bonsai.

◀ The sturdy, gnarled trunk reveals the old age of a spectacular azalea bonsai. Potted in a shallow container measuring 16 inches across, this type blooms eight months a year. Only the small-leaf varieties are suitable.

The first step for *Juniperus horizontalis*, bought in two-gallon container, is having its roots cleaned of soil and untangled (top). With shears, prune ⅓ of root mass from sides; ½ from bottom. Prune branches to conform.

Use two lengths of insulated copper wire. Bend end of first wire at right angle. Push it into the crown, then wrap upward around trunk. Insert second wire on opposite side; bring up to join first wire. Extend to wrap branches for shaping.

When wiring is completed, bend trunk and branches to desired positions (bottom). Use potting mixture of ⅓ sand, ⅓ peat, and ⅓ loam. In container of right size (with bottom drainage), tamp soil around roots. Anchor.

88

Mugho pine, planted in cascade style, is given off-center placement in a round container and displayed on a stand tall enough to permit the cascade to fall over the edge naturally.

This well-developed 10-year-old cutting of Japanese azalea has been trained in an upright style. Moss cover over potting soil helps to further the illusion of nature in miniature.

A low platform placed near a fence offers an ideal growing situation for a bonsai collection: part sun; and protection from strong wind.

Choosing the right plant is a vital factor in success with bonsai. It should, first, be suited to the climate of the area in which you live. In warm climates, deciduous varieties needing prolonged dormancy produced by cold weather are not feasible. In northern regions, tender varieties must be kept in a cool greenhouse or in a cold frame dug to a depth well below the frost line during all subfreezing weather.

Next, since a height of about three feet is considered the maximum for bonsai, you should select varieties that do not normally grow to immense heights. Dwarf and compact varieties are generally superior.

Since the final form sought is a miniature of nature that conveys the illusion of great age — never a grotesque distortion of nature — only fine-foliage types, with leaves that are in proportion to the plant, are suitable.

This dwarf variety of bamboo is relatively easy to train as a bonsai. Growth is regulated by frequently pinching off the tops. For flowering bonsai, pruning is done after blooming.

The use of redwood for bonsai stand makes it possible to water often without concern for protection of platform from damage by rot.

This Japanese red maple, about six years old, has been severely pruned to attain graceful contours in the slanting style. Maples require a cold period, as they are deciduous.

Once you've chosen the right plant, you must decide on a final form toward which you will train it. There are, as you see from examples pictured here, several classic categories: upright; slanting; and cascade. (The Japanese make further distinctions within some of these forms, which you may wish to pursue if you become an expert.)

IMPORTANCE OF DAILY CARE

Fascinating as bonsai are, it must be recognized that they are demanding plants and not for you if you're often away from home. Since they grow in minimal amounts of soil, they must be checked daily and watered as often as soil dries—which may also be daily. Nor do the tasks of training and pruning of bonsai end. They must be done as long as the plant continues to live.

English ivy *(Hedera helix)*, unusual among vining plants for the variety of leaf sizes and shapes in which it's available, is easy to grow if you supply the bright light it requires.

Evidence that the right location means healthy growth is this group of plants receiving filtered light from overhead, with watering made easy by setting pots on a bed of marble chips.

How to Grow Healthy Plants

A beginning indoor gardener hearing the old saying, "I don't have a green thumb," may conclude that success with plants involves a kind of magic. You may also have heard theories that talking to plants makes them grow! The scientific kernel of truth in such a mystical approach is that if you look daily at your plants (whether you talk to them or not), you'll be aware of their needs.

One way to ensure success is by choosing from those plants whose needs match the conditions you can provide. To help you do so, this chapter begins with a portfolio of recommended plants, grouped by requirements of light and humidity. Portfolio recommendations are supplemented by cultural information on plants pictured in earlier chapters.

The rest of the chapter deals with water, feeding, light, potting, and treatment of sick plants. Also covered are tips on vacation care and how to build or decorate inexpensive plant boxes and containers.

Inform yourself on needs of plants new to you, then check daily to see that you're meeting them. You'll soon be an 'expert.'

A portfolio of recommended house plants

low light/average humidity

To grow healthy house plants, it is necessary to supply the quantity of light and humidity that they require. As an aid in choosing wisely, consult the three categories that are presented in this section.

Attractive plants that can tolerate low light and humidity are included on these two pages (for others, see list on page 107). In the next group are plants needing medium to bright light and average humidity. In the third category are plants requiring higher humidity than the average home can supply

—plants to grow in a greenhouse or under lights, where humidity can be controlled.

The term 'low light' indicates a location where no direct light reaches a plant. (See also pages 106-107.) 'Medium light' indicates a spot near a window, not in sun. And 'bright' means near a window, receiving at least four or five hours of sun a day.

'Average humidity' means 30 percent; 'High' means 50 percent or more. (Consult pages 108-109 for recommended potting soil mixtures.)

Grape ivy (*Cissus rhombifolia*) is a vine that tolerates low light well (also grows well in part-sun). Use standard potting soil and keep moist. It roots readily from stem cuttings and is attractive in dish gardens and in hanging baskets. In a massed grouping, it can be trained on a trellis. Kangaroo vine (*C. antarctica*) is a relative that resembles it and takes similar culture. Its more colorful relative, *C. discolor*, needs higher humidity.

Jade plant (*Crassula argentea*) branches, grows old beautifully, and reaches a height of three feet or more. Preferred soil mixture contains half coarse sand or small pebbles; the other half, equal amounts of loam and peat. As for all succulents, the danger is in overwatering. During growth periods, water as you do an average house plant; when plant becomes semi-dormant (during winter), reduce water given and allow soil to become dry between waterings.

Norfolk Island pine (*Araucaria excelsa*), also called star pine, is one of the most admired and easily cared for house plants. It eventually reaches small-tree size. Kept in low light over a long period of time, spacing between tiers of branches becomes over-wide. A standard potting soil is recommended. Water as for other plants. Occasional misting is helpful. If you move plant outdoors in summer, it must be in a shaded situation.

Podocarpus macrophylla, which eventually attains small-shrub size, is an attractive pot plant at all stages, its dark green, slender leaves arranged in whorls around woody stems. Standard potting soil, evenly moist, is recommended. As a young plant, it is suitable for dish gardens; mature, grown in a large container, it is effective either as a single specimen, or used in a mass grouping of house plants to lend background height.

Rubber plant (*Ficus elastica*), as tough as it is handsome, is widely available in both solid green and white splashed foliage types. The white markings grow less distinct if the plant is constantly in low light. Reaches height of four or five feet. Use standard potting mixture, kept evenly moist in periods of growth (spring and summer). Allow soil to go quite dry between waterings in wintertime, when the rate of growth becomes much slower.

Umbrella plant (*Cyperus alternifolius*) grows to a height of four feet at maturity. Related to papyrus—the plant from which ancient Egyptians made paper—its main demand is for constantly damp soil, since it is a water plant in its natural state. Tips of leaves tend to turn brown, but they can be trimmed away without harm to the rest of the umbel of leaves of the plant. Another variety, less known *C. gracilis*, is smaller and more slender.

medium to bright light/ average humidity

On these and the following six pages of the portfolio, there are 31 plants to choose from, all of which will prosper in average home humidity (30 percent or more) and in medium to bright light. (For help in judging light quality, see pages 106-107.)

Some of these plants are striking enough to be grown as single specimens—important room accents. Others are desirable for the contrasts of form and leaf pattern they'll contribute to a massed planting or a smaller grouping of plants where variety is sought. A few are valued for seasonal bloom, but all have foliage interesting enough to make them worth growing all year-round.

Aeonium arboreum, a less-common succulent, is an arresting plant because of its treelike stem and neat gray green rosettes of foliage. It takes the same culture as other members of the succulent tribe (see jade plant, page 92) and grows to a height of about two feet. If the sculptured qualities of succulents interest you, grow them from seed. Packets of mixed succulent plant seed are inexpensive and germinate quite easily under light.

Aglaonema treubii is a handsomely variegated relative of the common Chinese evergreen. To retain leaf markings, it needs somewhat stronger light than does its solidly green relative. Use standard potting soil, kept constantly moist. Grow in medium to bright light. You can increase by root division or by stem cuttings taken from plants that grow overly tall. This variety, grown in good light, will not exceed from 8 to 10 inches in height.

Aloe Krapohliana, like all aloes, seldom needs repotting—every second or third year is sufficient. Its colorful spikes of orange and blue bloom appear in early winter. The plant is less than a foot tall at maturity. Grow it as any other succulent, reducing amount of water that you give it after flowering. So varied are the plants in the aloe family that they are a much-sought-after group to include in indoor gardens. Most put up red bloom in winter.

Aloe variegata is commonly called partridge breast because of its strong leaf patterns. It grows in rosettes that are triangular, and its leaves are edged and marbled sharply with white on dark green. This variety produces red flowers on spiky racemes about a foot tall. The plant itself reaches a height of from six to nine inches at maturity. Grow it as you do all succulents, avoiding overwatering. It requires medium to bright light in order to bloom.

Asparagus densiflorus is a vining plant whose feathery plumes of foliage offer flattering contrast to the shining, solid green leaves of such commonly grown house plants as the rubber plant or schefflera. Use standard potting soil, kept constantly moist. A more common relative, *A. Sprengerei,* can be used in similar ways. Both are suitable to grow in a hanging basket. Frequent misting keeps foliage attractive and promotes vigorous growth.

Carissa grandiflora horizontalis, dwarf relative of the natal plum (a tree) has a sprawling growth habit. Shiny, fleshy leaves grow in opposite and overlapping pairs on fairly woody stems. A large, fragrant white bloom appears at the tips of branches at irregular periods throughout the year, followed by big red berries that are long-lasting. Grow in a standard potting soil mixture, kept constantly moist, in bright light or full sun.

Dizygotheca elegantissima, a native of New Caledonia, is sometimes sold as 'aralia.' A shrub, it eventually grows four or five feet tall. Use standard potting soil mixture, making certain of good bottom drainage, since the plant requires ample water. Grow in medium to bright light, not sun. Slender, palmate leaves of coppery green recommend it for inclusion in mass plantings as contrast to big-leaf specimens, and for height in background placement.

Chenille plant (*Acalypha hispida*), its common name coming from furry texture of long red- or rose-colored tassels of bloom, flowers year-round. A tropical shrub, the plant dislikes cold, and, in winter, it should not be grown next to a window if temperature there drops below 65°. It prefers filtered light, not full sun. Use standard potting soil and keep moist. Plant is subject to mealybug, scale, and red spider mite. Check for these regularly.

Christmas cactus (both *Schlumbergera Bridgesii* and *Zygocactus truncatus* are referred to by this common name) is an easy-to-grow house plant that asks for special treatment only to guarantee bloom. When growth rate slows in early fall, it should be moved to a low-light situation, given no water for a period of four weeks (usually, the month of October). Return to normal light and water regularly in order to get bloom during the winter months.

Clivia, named for the Clive family of England, is a tender bulbous plant that produces showy red or coral flowers in large umbels in spring. Once a plant reaches blooming size, do not repot for several years, but fertilize regularly during growth period. A relative of the amaryllis, clivia maintains its stiff, straplike foliage in attractive condition throughout the year. Use standard potting soil mixture, and grow in bright light or full sun.

Cyanotis somaliensis resembles the tradescantia family in growth habits. Soft, hairy margins on shiny green leaves make this variety especially attractive. The plant creeps and is easily propagated by stem cuttings. *C. veldhoutiana*, a more colorful variety, has purple stems and leaf backs, thickly covered with soft, furry, white hairs. Grow these in a standard potting soil mixture in bright light. Let the soil become quite dry between waterings.

Davallia pentaphylla is one of a large family of ferny plants, some of them especially well suited to growing in hanging baskets. All of them prefer the cooler side of average house temperatures (preferably under 70°). They grow best in soil rich in organic material such as leaf mold, kept constantly moist. Spores borne in marginal rows on the backs of leaves will germinate under lights. Daily misting of the foliage—as for all ferns—is beneficial.

Exacum affine, little known to indoor gardeners, deserves wide popularity. It grows easily from seed, which can be sown in any month, with bloom to be expected about five months later. Flowers are somewhat fragrant, resembling the forget-me-not in color. Grow in standard potting soil, kept constantly moist, in medium to bright light or under artificial lights. The plant is a biennial, a member of the gentian family, and, when mature, is about 12 inches tall.

Fatshedera Lizei is a house plant hybrid that was produced by crossing the Japanese vine *Fatsia japonica* and *Hedera Helix* (English ivy). Use a standard potting soil mixture, keeping it constantly moist. As a young plant, fatshedera is bushy in habit, but, as it grows taller, it needs some support—a small trellis or bamboo plant stakes. Maintain lustrous dark green of five-lobed leaves with bright light. They prefer temperatures not over 70°.

Geraniums of the scented-leaf type are grown for their foliage as well as the perfume released as leaves are handled. Most, like this deeply cut and variegated specimen of peppermint geranium, produce rather unimpressive bloom, but their fragrances—rose, apple, ginger, cinnamon, lemon, and more—will compensate for lack of brilliant bloom characteristic of zonal geraniums. Grow in standard potting soil, on the dry side, in bright light.

Holly fern (*Cyrtomium falcatum rochefordianum*), native of Japan, gets its common name from the stiff, varnished look of its 8- to 10-inch fronds. It's easier to grow than the familiar Boston fern and makes less demand for high humidity. It grows well in medium or bright light, but not in full sun. Like the Boston fern, it's best grown in a standard potting soil mixture, kept moist. Spores are borne on the backs of leaves as brown dots. Subject to scale.

Hoya carnosa or wax plant is a twiner that needs support of a moss stick or small trellis. Umbels of fragrant bloom—white stars with pink centers—appear in summer. After bloom, don't remove spurs, as next year's buds arise there. Let plant go semidormant for the winter by moving to a cool, low-light situation. Reduce amount of water. In February, return to bright light and resume normal watering. Grow in standard potting soil, kept evenly moist.

Jerusalem Cherry (*Solanum pseudo-capsicum*) is valued for its long-lasting, bright orange fruits (*not* edible). To grow from seed, allow fruit to ripen on plant. Sow seed indoors in March, handling as you would tomatoes. After frost danger is past, sink pots—one plant per pot—in a sunny garden spot. Bring indoors to bright light or full sun in early fall for flowering and fruit at holidays. Grows to two feet. Use standard potting soil, kept moist, not wet.

Joseph's Coat (*Alternanthera*) is a colorful foliage plant widely grown in outdoor gardens but well suited to house plant culture. It roots easily from stem cuttings, or can be grown from seed. Use standard potting soil mixture, kept moist. Grow in bright light or full sun. It also does well under artificial light. Mature plant will reach 8 to 12 inches in height. Foliage contains colorful mixtures of cream, rose, red, purple, and green. Good in dish gardens.

Kalanchoe blossfeldiana flowers profusely in early winter with red orange umbels of bloom. New hybrids are six to eight inches tall. A succulent, it produces its own crop of plant- lets if leaves dropping on surface of soil are allowed to root. Or reproduce by rooting the leaves as for African violets. (See page 52.) Use standard potting soil and grow in bright light or under artificial light. Allow soil surface to become quite dry between waterings.

Oxalis ortgiesii is distinguished from other hybrids of its group by red-tinged foliage. Most are green. Grown primarily for foliage, it blooms in spring, with small yellow flowers on stems a bit taller than its 16- to 18-inch height. Most hybrids are from 6 to 10 inches tall. Color of bloom in various hybrids includes white, pink, and crimson. Use standard potting soil, kept moist. It grows well under artificial light or in medium to bright light.

Ornamental grasses, seldom found in indoor gardens, deserve attention for their use in dish gardens, planters, and groupings of house plants for the contrast they offer. The variety pictured, *Acorus gramineus variegatus*, has white markings on slender 8- to 10-inch foliage. Blue-eyed grass (*Sisyrinchium bellum*) 9 inches, and Hare's-tail grass (*Lagurus ovatus*) 12 inches, are others grown indoors. Grow in medium to bright light and in standard soil.

Peperomia obtusifolia variegata is a member of a sizable plant family deserving attention for variety of foliage. Emerald Ripple and Water- melon peperomia, as well as the solid green variety of the plant pictured, are a few worth using in dish gardens or as single specimens. All of those mentioned reach from 8 to 10 inches in height. Grow the peperomias in standard potting soil, in medium or bright light. Allow soil to dry between waterings.

Philodendron panduriforme, a member of a valued group of ornamental plants, mostly of climbing nature, is also called 'fiddle-leaf' philodendron because of its three-lobed foliage. A fairly rapid growing variety, it's well suited for training on a moss stick. Use a standard potting soil mixture and grow it in medium light. To start a new vine, take a sturdy tip cutting and root in water, coarse sand, or one of the growing mediums.

Philodendron squamiferum, its leaves glossier than the fiddle-leaf variety pictured at left, has the same vining tendencies and takes the same culture. Worth exploring also are some of the 'self-heading' varieties of philodendron that have less vining tendency. Among the most handsome are : *P. selloum,* its leaves deeply lobed; *P. bipinnatifidum,* almost fernlike; *P. erubescens,* with a reddish cast to foliage; and *P. sodiroi,* mottled leaf.

Pineapple plants, often sold in supermarkets at inexpensive prices, are members of the bromeliad tribe (see pages 83-85) and require similar culture. It's possible to grow your own by cutting into the top of a pineapple you buy to eat and removing crown of foliage along with 2- to 3-inch core, rooting in coarse sand or in a growing medium such as vermiculite. Expect to wait up to two years for fruit. Grow in medium or bright light.

Portulacaria afra, which resembles the jade plant, is more branched and has daintier fleshy leaves. It is less tolerant of insufficient light and should be grown in brightest light obtainable. As for all succulent plants, overwatering is a major danger. Use standard potting soil, allowing surface soil to become quite dry to the touch between waterings. It is easy to propagate this plant by making stem cuttings from side branches and rooting in coarse sand.

Screw pine, of the pandanus family, is a handsome house plant with spirally arranged foliage, each spearlike leaf edged with prickly
teeth. The variety pictured, *P. veitchii,* is
strongly marked with white and grows to a
height of 18 to 24 inches. Other hybrids have
varying degrees of variegation. These plants
like as much warmth as possible (75° or higher)
and bright light during main growth period
(winter through spring). Mist daily.

Spathiphyllum floribundum, its botanical
name referring to white leaflike spathes that
are thought of as flowers, looks a bit like the
calla lily, but it is not—as calla lilies are—a
bulb plant. These plants prefer the upper
ranges of house temperatures (75° or higher)
and are tolerant of average humidity. Use a
standard potting soil mixture, kept constantly
moist. Grow in medium light. Bloom appears
in late spring or early summer.

Trileaf Wonder, the commercial name of this
member of the syngonium family, its foliage
generously marbled with creamy-white, is an
excellent plant to use in dish gardens, but
interesting enough to deserve attention even
when grown singly. Related hybrids, all having the characteristic arrowhead-shaped foliage, are also variegated in differing degrees.
Grow in standard potting soil mixture, kept
moist. Medium light is best.

Veltheimia, an unusual but easy-to-grow, tender bulbous plant, puts up tall stalks of pink-
and green-tipped bloom from a rosette of
glossy, straplike foliage during early spring.
Grow in standard potting soil mixture, kept
constantly moist, in medium or bright light.
When bloom period ends, shift plant to cool,
dark location for semidormant condition during summer, watering occasionally. In early
fall, return to light and resume watering.

medium to bright light/high humidity

Most of the house plant exotics pictured and described here are best grown either in a cool greenhouse, under artificial lights where high humidity is maintained, in glass-enclosed view gardens like the one pictured on page 88, or, when young, in a terrarium. The key to success for all of them is humidity — much higher than average homes supply in winter: 50 percent or higher.

Several of the plants shown here — aucuba, aphelandra, and croton — are frequently sold as young plants at reasonable prices. If you admire them but cannot maintain the conditions necessary for growth, buy one, place it where needs can be met as closely as possible, and consider it as you would cut flowers — to be enjoyed, then discarded.

Aphelandra, an extremely showy plant, is remarkable for white-veined, shiny foliage and gaudy bloom spikes that normally appear during autumn. Of several varieties in cultivation, *A. squarrosa louisae* (its bloom is a vivid yellow) is the one commonly sold by florists. Except in a cool greenhouse maintaining humidity over 50 percent and temperatures of 50° to 70°, it's difficult to produce bloom or keep foliage attractive. Needs diffused light.

Asplenium myriophyllum, a lacy fern, puts up fronds of 6 to 15 inches and is suitable to grow in a cool greenhouse (see description under aphelandra), except that the plant has a tendency to turn brown during winter if humidity is excessive. It requires good light, but never direct exposure to sun. In the greenhouse, the plant should get some shade. A good potting mixture contains half rich garden loam and half leaf mold for retaining moisture.

Aucuba japonica piturata, an ornamental shrub in southern gardens, is best grown in a cool greenhouse in the north, or under artificial light if high humidity is maintained and growth lamps (stronger wattage than fluorescents) are used. Gold-splashed leaves of smooth, shiny surface make it a good companion to lacy- or furry-leaved plants. Half sand and half rich garden loam make an excellent potting mixture. Grow in medium light.

Croton (correct botanical name is *Codiaeum*), much admired for vivid foliage colors including red, orange, yellow, pink, brown, as well as many shadings of green, is another decorative shrub quite often seen in tropical gardens. Elsewhere, it's a greenhouse plant needing high humidity (without it, leaves drop) and bright light (in too dim light all new leaves will be green). Grow in standard potting soil mixture, kept evenly moist.

Gardenia jasminoides, Cape jasmine, blooms reliably in winter, making it a more desirable house plant than the shrub form that blooms in southern gardens during spring and summer. The flowers are smaller than the florists' variety, but have the same fragrance and velvety texture of petals. A major problem—buds dropping—is lessened if the plant is grown in acid soil (rich in peat and leaf mold) at even temperatures (65° to 75°).

Hibiscus rosa-sinensis, long a favorite conservatory plant, reaches three to eight feet when container grown; as a subtropical shrub, it may even reach 30 feet. Hybrids now available produce red, yellow, rose, pink, or white bloom of impressive size. Each bloom lasts only a day, but the plant is almost everblooming in greenhouse conditions of bright light and high humidity. Grow in standard potting soil mixture, kept constantly moist.

Pilea berterlonia, sold as 'Moon Valley,' is a compact plant with deeply veined and attractively colored foliage that can be grown either in a light garden using the plant growth lamps and maintaining 50 percent humidity or in a greenhouse, in diffused light. A more widely known relative, *P. cadierei*, or 'aluminum plant,' so-called because of silver markings on leaves, requires same growing conditions. Use standard potting soil, kept moist.

Watering/feeding

"How often shall I water or feed my house plant?" is the question most often asked by beginning indoor gardeners. The correct answer, "That depends..." is not so satisfying as a rule-of-thumb reply like "once a week" might be, but it's the only accurate advice that can be given for house plants.

For example, your home in winter may be almost as arid as a desert. If so, your plants will need more water than during warm, humid summer weather. Likewise, plants in small pots probably will need watering more often than those in large pots—the smaller pot dries out faster. But, while a plant in bloom needs more water than it does at other times, in general, variations in water needs from plant to plant aren't great. Except for cactus and succulents, most plants grow best in soil that is constantly moist—*not* wet.

A good rule: water whenever the topsoil feels dry—whether daily or weekly. Also, water thoroughly, so to supply enough water to moisten the soil all the way to the bottom.

If you water from the top, be sure to have broken potsherds, pebbles, or other loose material at the bottom of the pot for good drainage. This is not necessary for bottom watering. Instead, insert a wick (preferably one of fiber glass) to absorb water from a dish below, keeping soil moist.

Whether you water from top or bottom, it's good practice to give plants an occasional 'dunking.' Place the pot in a pail, or in your kitchen sink filled so that the pot will be half submerged. When the surface of the soil is moist, set the plant aside and allow the surplus water to drain away. Then return the plant to its usual location. (In the process, it's a good idea to syringe the foliage and remove dust at the same time.)

However, don't leave the pot standing in water more than an hour. Too much water over a long period prevents oxygen from getting to the roots—roots must have oxygen.

For most plants (succulents and cactus are exceptions) it's almost impossible to overwater if you've provided adequate drainage.

When you water from the top, add enough water so the excess drains out at the bottom. This ensures moistening *all* the soil. Use a saucer to catch drainage, and empty it when necessary to keep pot from standing in water.

Special self-watering flowerpots have a built-in reservoir that feeds water to soil through a wick. You can devise one with a fiber glass wick, disk to hold pot above water, and a deep dish to hold the water supply.

A common mistake made by amateur indoor gardeners is overfertilizing. A little plant food goes a long way—too much can burn the roots and actually kill a plant. This is especially important to watch, for the various brands of fertilizers on the market differ in strength. So it pays to follow package directions exactly.

How much food you give your plants is also influenced by the seasons of the year. While older plants benefit from a light feeding every few weeks, during winter it is best to stop feeding them except those that bloom during this period. Most of the foliage plants grown as house plants go into a reduced growth period during colder months, and giving them fertilizer disturbs their natural growth habits. You should also guard against fertilizing new plants obtained from your florist. They need no fertilizer for the first six weeks after you buy them—in fact, feeding these plants may be harmful to them.

Commercial fertilizers always indicate on the package the proportions of nutrients they contain. Those usually present are nitrogen, phosphoric acid, and potash, generally represented on packages and in the order stated by the ratio figures.

In your eagerness to help your plants along, you may overdo your feeding. It's not wise to assume that any sickly looking plant will benefit from a dose of plant food. The plant is more apt to be ailing because of too little light, too much or too little water, too dry an atmosphere, or poor quality of potting soil.

If your plant *is* suffering from starvation, nitrogen is most likely to be what it lacks. Symptoms are a yellow color in new leaves, and lack of vigor in new growth.

While symptoms of injury from gas fumes, too much water and too little light are similar, when one of these is the culprit you usually find lower leaves turning yellow, while those higher up stay green.

Plant foods come in powdered, granulated, tablet, and liquid form. Experiment with all kinds, following suggestions below, to see which plant food you prefer.

When using dry food, be careful not to get it on the plant, and to water into the soil at once. Tablets may be inserted in the soil at the outer edge of pot. These are absorbed in the course of several waterings.

The main thing to remember about fertilizers is "Don't kill a plant with kindness!"

Water dry food into soil at once to prevent possible burning. Regular lawn food works fine; half a teaspoon to a 6-inch pot is the right amount. Apply commercial house plant food exactly as the package directions state.

When you use liquid plant food in solution, be sure to measure the water just as accurately as you do the food. Use enough of the solution to moisten all soil—until the excess drains out at the bottom of the pot.

Light

Houses are built for people—not plants. By a plant's standards, houses are too dark, too dry, and often too hot—like sunless deserts. The wonder is that so many plants survive.

Light needs of plants have received careful study by scientists in recent years. The amateur indoor gardener now has at his command the results of their research.

The chart at the bottom of the page and the photographs of typical home situations at right will help you to determine how much light plants in your home are actually receiving when measured in footcandles.

Scientists use the unit, 'footcandle,' to denote quantity of illumination. Technically, one footcandle is equal to the amount of illumination cast on an object by one candle at a distance of one foot. Light meters used for photographic purposes measure light on the object to be photographed, rather than the strength of the light itself. But, with a chart that some manufacturers can supply, these photographic light meter readings can be converted to the footcandle units plant experts refer to. Or, much handier, there is now on the market a pocket-sized meter made especially for the purpose of measuring the amount of light available to plants. It has a range of from 0 to 5000 footcandles.

What happens when a plant gets too little light? Nothing, at first. Plants can survive for long periods on reserve food. Ultimately, however, new growth becomes spindly, new leaves smaller, and lower leaves die.

It may take only a few weeks, or as long as a year for a plant to show symptoms of light starvation. The cure is not a massive dose of light—this could kill a plant—but a return to adequate light conditions.

Nor is it wise to set foliage plants next to unshaded windows that face directly into the sun except during the coldest winter months. Even then, with the reflected light from snow, the total could be excessive. Very few foliage plants can tolerate direct sunlight, especially when magnified by clear glass. Shifted to such a spot from a dim corner, they will sunburn.

There are several ways you can give your plants more light safely: by moving them a little closer to windows, by moving them to a brighter room, or by leaving draperies and blinds open during the daylight hours. The most convenient way is to supplement the natural light available with artificial light.

There are several ways to supply proper light. You can use incandescent lamps, fluorescent tubes, or special growth lamps to

HOMES		Conference room	30 footcandles
General illumination	5 footcandles*		
Reading or writing	20 footcandles	STORES	
Ironing and sewing	40 footcandles	Circulation areas	20 footcandles
Workbench	40 footcandles	Merchandising areas	50 footcandles
		Displays	100 to 200 footcandles
HOTELS			
Lobby	20 footcandles	OUTDOORS	
Dining room	5 to 10 footcandles	Bright, summer day	
			About 10,000 footcandles
OFFICES		Cloudy, winter day	
Typing, accounting	50 footcandles		500 to 2,000 footcandles

*Amount of illumination at all points—one foot from a uniform point source of one international candle.

Low light: away from windows or other source of daylight (top). Choose plants tolerant of 25 to 300 footcandle minimum daily, such as aspidistra, and sanseveria species.

Medium light: next to window, but, if a south window, sunlight is diffused through curtains (bottom left). Choose plants needing 300 to 700 footcandles minimum: ferns, and begonias.

High light: next to uncurtained south window (bottom right). Grow plants here needing 700 to 1000 footcandles daily: English ivy and forced spring bulbs being brought into flower.

supplement sunlight. Ceiling spotlights can be a successful light source, too, and they are decorative as well as functional in supplying general lighting for one area of a room. (For a more complete discussion of growing plants with the aid of artificial light, see the section on this subject on pages 74-79.)

There is still another trick employed by clever indoor gardeners who wish to use a plant for a major decorative role but find that the best location has insufficient light. This is to buy two specimens of the particular plant you want, and shift the two periodically from the spot where the plant performs best decoratively to the location where the light is ideal. This shifting should take place on a weekly basis (or more often) in order to keep both plants healthy over as long a period as possible.

If the plant in question is a large one—a tubbed palm, totem-style monstera, or other plant that is four or five feet tall—it is a heavy job to shift the plant from one place to another. This problem can often be solved by displaying the plants on low platforms equipped with casters, thus, reducing the physical exertion to a minimum when the time arrives to shift the two. Such platforms on wheels are available commercially, but they are simple enough to build so that almost any handyman can easily put one together —at a total cost of only a few dollars.

Potting/repotting

Whether you begin with a seedling, a rooted cutting, a plant lifted from the garden, or a bulb, the way you first pot a plant is vital to its future health. Pot it incorrectly, and chances of it growing well are slim.

Most important is the quality of the potting soil in which your plant will grow. With few exceptions, house plants thrive in a potting soil mixture composed of gravel, peat, and soil in equal proportions—as illustrated in the top left drawing across the page.

Exceptions to this are: cactus and succulents of most kinds, which grow best in a mixture of half soil and half coarse sand; ferns, which prefer a mixture of half soil and half leaf mold or sphagnum moss; and a few house plants, such as camellias, which need an acid soil and acid fertilizer. These are available at garden shops everywhere.

You can make up your own potting soil mixture, or you can buy it commercially prepared. But whatever kind of mixture that you use, be sure it is moist—not dry or wet—when you're ready to use it. Tender roots 'settle in' best and suffer the least damage in moist soil. It's handy to keep some soil that's properly damp in a plastic bag.

Don't forget to put a layer of coarse material for drainage in the bottom of the pot before you begin to fill with potting soil. Broken chunks of clay pots or small rocks are good for this purpose. Omit this step if you use a self-watering pot.

Consider looks, too, when you pot a plant. Your eye will tell you when a pot is of the correct size, in proportion to the plant. Clay pots come in sizes up to 14 inches. The standard size has a depth equal to top diameter; the sizes called 'bulb' and 'azalea' pans are not as deep as they are wide.

If the plant is young and of a type that can be expected to grow rapidly, allow for this future growth in selecting the size of the pot. If you choose one too small, repotting will soon be necessary.

If you use a pot in which plants have previously grown, make certain that it is thoroughly clean before reusing it.

A plant needs repotting when its roots get matted around the outside of the soil ball in which it is growing. Fast-growing plants should be checked every three or four months. Slow-growing plants probably will not need repotting more than once a year.

Ordinarily, it is best to shift a plant to a pot no more than an inch or two larger than its former pot. If the pot is too large in relation to the plant, the soil will dry out very slowly and it will be difficult for you to control the moisture. Topsoil may be dry while central soil is still wet.

As a further aid to good watering practices, most beginners should use clay pots rather than plastic ones, since plastic pots permit no respiration through sides, and it is easy to misjudge and overwater when relying on topsoil as the indicator. Plant growers and shippers often use plastic pots because of their light weight and low breakage rate. But these factors are no longer relevant when you grow plants in your home.

Normally, the roots of a plant need not be disturbed at all when you set it into a larger pot. Simply add fresh potting soil at the bottom, the sides, and the top. But if the original soil ball has become packed down, has had poor drainage, or has had too many soluble salts (from hard water), then all of the soil should be removed and replaced. Do this gently, after having watered thoroughly on the day preceding repotting so as to damage roots as little as possible. Spread the roots as you sift the fresh potting soil around them.

Beginners are tense about damaging plants in the course of repotting, but it is really a simple operation to perform without injuring a plant. Always water on the day before you repot so that all of the soil ball will be uniformly moistened.

Follow the steps pictured on the facing page, making certain that you support the plant with one hand while tapping it out of the pot. And always leave a thumb's width of space free below the rim of the pot to allow for future watering.

Standard potting mixture (top) is: ⅓ gravel for drainage; ⅓ peat to hold water, nutrients; garden or other good soil makes up the remaining third. Make your own or buy it.

After putting in coarse material for drainage (middle), fill soil in gently around tender roots. When pot is full, thump on solid surface to firm soil down; leave room to water.

Water all newly potted plants thoroughly. Set in spot where plant receives light but not bright sun until after it has become adjusted —not for two or three days after potting.

To remove plant from pot (top), place fingers of one hand over soil ball. Turn pot upside down. Tap sharply on table edge. Plant will slide out. Matted roots mean repotting's due.

Cover hole in pot (middle) with bottle cap or bits of broken pot to keep soil from washing out. If pot is over four inches deep, a layer of gravel at the bottom will improve drainage.

Set plant in new pot to test whether size is right. Add soil to bring to right height. Fill around roots with soil. Press firmly with your thumbs. Water and keep out of sun.

First aid for sick plants

The major reasons why some house plants do not flourish are: **(1)** too much or too little light; **(2)** too much or too little water; **(3)** too low or too high humidity; **(4)** improper potting soil; **(5)** too high or too low temperatures; **(6)** too much or too little feeding; and **(7)** insects and diseases.

Light: Insufficient light over a long period manifests itself in spindly stems, yellow green foliage color, and leaf drop. Eventually, all growth stops and the plant dies.

Plants in the home seldom get an overdose of light. If, however, they've been accustomed to filtered light and you move them into a sunny window, leafburn or paling of foliage may soon become noticeable.

Different plants require varying amounts of light. In general, foliage plants can survive with much less light than those that produce bloom. If you choose the right plant for the light you can offer, you'll have few light troubles. (For more information, consult sections on light and on growing plants under artificial light, as well as the portfolio section (pages 92-103) and individual plant listings in this book.)

Water: If a plant receives too little water, it wilts. However, this seldom causes serious damage unless it occurs frequently; then, it stunts growth and causes flower drop.

Too much water is a more common problem. The first symptom is usually dropping of lower leaves. New leaves may continue to appear on top, but an overwatered plant gets leggy and bare of foliage at the base.

If you suspect that a plant has had too much water, tap it out of its pot and look at the roots. Root tips should be white. If they are brown, remove soil and repot in loose, spongy soil. Water less frequently.

Humidity: Few house plants suffer from too much humidity. Average homes have humidity readings of 30 percent and less in the coldest months—insufficient for many plants.

Heavy scale infestation, such as is shown on a holly fern, will not occur if you inspect frequently. Treat scale promptly with spray specifically designed for the purpose, applied according to the manufacturer's directions.

Cottony-white mealybugs find African violets a favorite victim. Dilute alcohol with equal parts of water. Use a toothpick wrapped in cotton to touch each insect with solution. Follow with a thorough rinse of lukewarm water spray.

Raise humidity with a cool vapor humidifier or by setting pots in a waterproof tray, on a layer of pebbles, with the water level kept below the top of the pebbles. Signs of too little humidity are browning of leaf tips and margins, and, with flowering plants, bud drop and failure to produce bloom.

Potting soil: Consult pages 108-109 for information on standard mixture and other mixtures recommended for house plants.

Temperature: Most house plants tolerate average home temperatures ranging from 60° to 75°. (Check individual listings for special needs of the plants that you grow.)

Feeding: Most plants go into a semidormant or reduced growth period during the winter months. (A few are dormant at other times.) They should not be fed during those periods. (See page 105 and specific plant listings for additional information.)

Insects and diseases: Plants that are grown indoors are seldom attacked by either insects or diseases if you buy them from a reputable florist or greenhouse grower. The only disease—as distinct from infestation by insects—that occurs often enough to consider

here is caused by soil-borne, rot-producing organisms. In young plants, it is known as 'damping off.' In older plants, it is called 'stem rot.' To make sure that the potting soil you prepare is not infected, bake the moist soil mixture at 250° for 1½ hours in a closed metal container. As there is no effective remedy, plants having this disease should be destroyed promptly.

WHAT TO DO ABOUT INSECTS

Those insects that attack house plants can be effectively controlled with the same chemicals that are used to eliminate similar garden pests if the manufacturer's precautions are strictly observed.

To prevent pests from getting a start, clean plants often by syringing in the sink or by cleaning foliage with a soft, damp cloth. Use lukewarm water; support each leaf with one hand as you wipe the top with the other.

If you do notice pests such as mealybugs, red spiders, or scale, isolate the plant at once and treat it as suggested in pictures and text at the bottom of these pages.

Red spiders and mealybugs seldom become a problem if you give plants a twice-a-year wash with soapy water, followed by a clear water rinse. If insects are found, follow cleanup with application of appropriate insecticide.

When you check a plant, turn the leaves over and look at undersides—the place where most insects are actively at work. Mealybugs on plant at right can easily be eradicated by a soap bath, clear rinse, and insecticide spray.

Outdoor locations for house plants

A summer out of doors is of real benefit to most house plants. Nearly all of them like the brighter light that they can get on a shaded porch or on a patio. Almost no house plant, however, likes full sun. Most of them need protection from strong wind and beating rain and are not well suited to growing in an open garden border.

Shown on the opposite page and on the two that follow are a variety of summer locations that are congenial to the majority of house plants. Use these ideas as a guide in arranging an outdoor summer location for your collection of house plants—or for as much of it as can profit from the move.

A first precaution is never to move any house plants to an outdoor location until the temperature can be relied upon not to sink below the minimum acceptable to tender varieties—55° to 60°. June is the earliest safe time in most northern areas.

Check carefully to learn the position of the sun at various times of day. A spot that seems ideal in morning hours may become far too sunny for most foliage plants by midday or afternoon. Therefore, it's unwise to put plants in locations that will require shifting at certain hours during each day. One error in memory, and your favorite—a prized plant— can be completely ruined by leafburn.

If you like to slip clay pots inside decorative metal or ceramic containers, make certain rain will not fall directly onto a plant, fill up an outer container with water, and waterlog the soil, causing root rot.

Unless your summer vacation spot for house plants is screened, you must check much more often for insect infestation. If it

◀ A corrugated plastic roof filters sunlight on plants that move outdoors for the summer. The slatted background fence permits air circulation but protects against strong breezes.

occurs, treat promptly with appropriate insecticide, following manufacturer's instructions. And always check such plants before you bring them indoors at summer's end.

Remember that your watering schedule will differ from the one that you maintained indoors. Strong winds and hot, dry weather mean frequent waterings; conversely, prolonged rainy spells when humidity is high call for longer intervals between waterings.

TIPS ON VACATION CARE
Whether you move plants outdoors for the summer or keep them indoors year-round, you face the problem of keeping plants watered when you're off on vacation.

In the case of large and valuable plants, an indoor location is best no matter what the season of your vacation, since a sudden change in weather will not matter. A thorough watering followed by enclosing the entire plant in a plastic tent (leave some gaps for air circulation) keeps most plants supplied with moisture for about two weeks. Be sure to insert stakes so that the plastic does not touch the foliage, and place the plant away from direct sunlight.

For smaller plants, the same technique can be employed. Or, you can double pot. In this method, you set the pot into another one several sizes larger, and pack the space between with well-dampened sphagnum. This, too, will keep the average plant in good condition for a period of two weeks.

If your vacation is longer than two weeks, either ask someone to come in to water at times specified by you or 'farm out' your plants to friends who will take good care of them in your absence.

In the case of large and expensive plants purchased from a local greenhouse, it is sometimes possible—for a reasonable fee— to arrange to have your plant picked up and cared for in the greenhouse during your absence and returned when you come home.

Fiberboard panels with a lattice-work pattern screen a patio from the driveway view and offer a sheltered location for house plants hung from rafters or displayed on shelves. Fiber glass roof filters sun and keeps out rain.

Lath screen admits light and air for a group of plants. The 10x7-foot divider starts with four pairs of 2x4 supports anchored in ready-mix concrete. A combination of ½x½-inch and 1x½-inch laths makes the design.

In a long-established garden where tall trees shade a sheltered patio, plants in stands and arranged on a brick floor receive protection from sun and strong wind. Other plants are shaded by a tree at the far side of patio.

A weather-resistant, aluminum, lean-to garden house has lath and screen sides and mesh screen overhead to let in light and breeze.

House plants find a safely sheltered summer location on shelves ranged along one side, with house plant supplies conveniently at hand.

Strips of lath (three longer ones serve as legs) were nailed to three circles of plywood for a contour planter (right). Cut hole in top piece to fit pot; leave middle one solid. Stain.

Transform everyday pots with yarn you use to tie up gifts (below left). Paint lower half of pot with glue. Wrap yarn around and press into place. Treat top half in same manner.

Floral-fabric covering on a plastic pot begins by glueing top inch of fabric on side up to rim (below right). Make vertical cuts every two inches. Stretch and overlap fabric.

Varied lengths of cane fishing poles make an unusual trim for this planter (bottom). Drill hole in end of each piece and run wire or fish cord through holes. Staple cord ends to top rim.

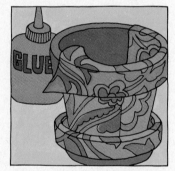

Containers to make or trim

Even the simplest of plants can look new and stylish in a decorative container. Although costly to buy, plant boxes, stands, and cover-ups for clay or plastic pots are yours for bargain prices if you supply the labor.

In the case of outdoor plant boxes, it's quite important to use durable materials and finishes that are weatherproof. Sun, wind, and rain can quickly destroy the looks of less sturdy ones. Redwood, of course, weathers beautifully; it won't rot when exposed to rain and dampness. If you use less expensive wood, apply protective finishes and stains to prolong its life.

For indoor pot cover-ups, you can be as carefree in the use of color as you like, although few plants except green foliage plants can hold their own next to colors as brilliant as the reds and blues shown here. For flowering plants, substitute shades of green, brown, or gray instead of the more brilliant hues that steal the show in a contest with pale pastel bloom.

Besides the clay pots and diminutive versions of bushel baskets, try trimming the throw-away plastic and metal containers your groceries come in or inexpensive waste-baskets. (For more ideas on inexpensive ways to wrap gift plants, see pages 66-67.)

Use ¾-inch exterior-grade plywood to make a tall plant box (top). Coat inside with liquid fiber glass. Face with prefab screen panels. Spacer dowels hold ¾x1⅝-inch boards apart.

Two unpainted white paper paint buckets (bottom left), separated by plastic-foam pedestal (available at floral and hobby shops), provide a budget-cost cover-up for clay pots.

Miniature bushel baskets big enough to hold a large pot are available in several colors (bottom right). Give one a beauty treatment with glued-on velvet ribbons in contrasting colors.

Seed

Asparagus fern	Gloxinia
Avocado	Impatiens
Bromeliads	Lemon
Cactus	Kalanchoe
Coleus	Orange
	Succulents

Root division

Aspidistra	Echeveria
Airplane plant	English ivy
Boston fern	Maranta
Chinese evergreen	Pandanus
Devil's ivy	Peperomia
	Sansevieria

Leaf cutting

African violet	Philodendron*
Gloxinia	Rex begonia
Kalanchoe*	Sansevieria
Peperomia	Scindapsus*
	Sedum species

*Cutting must include a leaf bud and leaf.

Stem cutting

Christmas cactus	Grape-ivy
Coleus	Impatiens
Crown of thorns	Nephthytis
Dracaena	Peperomia
English ivy	Rubber plant
	Velvet plant

Runners or offsets
African violet
Airplane plant
Apostle plant
Asparagus fern
—or any plant you

Boston fern
Bromeliads (some species)
Orchids (some species)
Pick-a-back plant
Strawberry saxifrage
can start by division

Air-layering
Croton
Dieffenbachia
Dracaena
—or any plant that you can start by means of
a stem cutting.

Fatshedera
Fiddle-leaf fig
Jade plant
Rubber plant

How to Multiply Your Plants

Everyone who develops more than a passing interest in house plants wants to try his hand at propagating new ones. The easiest and most common way to do this is by making a stem cutting, for there are few house plants that do not respond to this method.

Root division is the second most frequent method of propagation. Plants that send up a number of branches at the surface of the pot can almost always be cut into several portions; then, each part can be potted individually as a new plant.

Growing house plants from seed—unlike growing plants for the garden—is the least used method. Without a light setup, it is difficult in ordinary home surroundings to keep temperatures low enough and supply sufficient humidity for growth of the seedlings. If you can overcome these obstacles, it's an inexpensive way to grow plants in quantity, and to obtain varieties that might otherwise be hard to find.

Use the pictures and text in this chapter to learn how to handle each of the six methods of plant propagation with success.

Seed

The list of house plants that you can grow from seed is a long one. Increasing your plant collection this way costs pennies per plant in comparison with the dollars it takes to buy established specimens of many varieties from your florist or greenhouse.

Growing plants from seed takes patience; most plants will not reach display size for many months. You will also have to supply the growing conditions needed to germinate seed and to bring them to mature size.

Starting house plants from seed can be done on a small or large scale, depending on the space that you can devote to it and the number of plants you want. A 6-inch pot will easily accommodate 10 seedlings. For large quantities, or for starting a variety of new plants at one time, it's more efficient to use a flat, as pictured across the page.

To grow new plants, use these: a plastic sheet to trap humidity; sphagnum moss and vermiculite for air-layering; vermiculite or sand to root cuttings, or start seed; and varying proportions of sand, soil, and peat to suit the particular needs of the new plants.

Seed companies sell seed in quantities as small as three, four, or five for such exotics as clivia, croton, and anthurium, with price per seed ranging from 5 to 15 cents. The seed of unusual geraniums, African violets, many choice gesneriads, and the new dwarf gloxinias are usually sold in larger quantities, but the price per plant that you grow from a seed remains low.

For the first stage, besides seed, you need vermiculite, perlite, coarse sand, finely screened sphagnum moss, or other growing medium. Generally, soil is not recommended for germinating seed since danger of bacteria that causes 'damping off' is considerably higher with soil than with the other materials listed above. Whatever the medium that you decide to use, you must keep it uniformly moist (never wet) during germination. This ranges from a few days to a few weeks, depending on the variety of plant.

For the second stage—when seedlings show first true leaves or are about an inch tall—you'll need a flat or a number of 2-inch pots and a light soil mixture consisting of equal parts of sharp sand or gravel, peat, and garden soil. Add compost to this mixture if it is available, but don't feed newly transplanted seedlings until growth is further along. In two or three weeks you can use fertilizer diluted in water according to the manufacturer's directions. If you first transplant seedlings to a flat, you must pot each separately in a 2-inch pot by the time plants are three to four inches tall.

While the plants are growing in 2-inch pots, check the water needs daily, making certain that the soil never dries out entirely. As for all plants, subsequent repotting should be done whenever the root ball completely fills the pot. Shift to a pot no more than one or two sizes larger than the one in which it was previously grown.

An artificial light setup is ideal, though not essential for growing house plants from seed. If the light is overhead, the young plants grow straight; they won't lean toward the light as they do when grown in windows. With a light setup, it is easier to maintain high humidity during germination, since you can drape plastic over the light fixture to keep trapped air humid.

If you use fine-shredded sphagnum as the medium for germinating seed, it should first be uniformly moistened, then tamped down in flat with a brick or block of wood so that the surface is level. Use the same technique when preparing a flat of potting soil into which you transplant seedlings. Leave room to water.

After preparing a flat of potting soil as described above, use a strip of lath or a ruler to press in evenly spaced rows where the young plants will be grown. Do not overcrowd, as you must provide for further growth. Allow four square inches of space per plant.

When you grow a variety of seed in one flat, insert identifying plant labels. Use glass or plastic to cover flat until germination begins. Remove immediately thereafter to avoid damping off. If light's too strong for germination, cover flat with paper during this period.

As seed germinates (bottom left), inspect daily to make certain growing medium stays moist, and to thin out weaklings. Also shift seedlings growing too close to their neighbors. Use a pencil or dibble to pry up the seedlings without damage to their tender roots.

When first true leaves appear (bottom right), transplant to a flat filled with potting mixture, or into individual 2-inch pots. Make a hole in the soil with pencil or dibble so the roots can be set in place easily. Firm soil about the roots and water the plant well immediately. Keep out of any bright light for several days.

Stem cutting

Stem cutting is the most common method of plant propagation. While the majority of stem cuttings root easily in water, water-grown roots are much more brittle and are more apt to break off in the process of potting than are roots grown in vermiculite or one of the other nonorganic rooting mediums. To prepare and root stem cuttings, follow pictures and text on this page.

Use a sharp knife (below) to make a cutting from 4- to 6-inches long, *not longer*. Make cut just below point where leaf joins stem (roots develop best there). Remove lower leaves so as to have bottom inch or two of stem bare.

Fill a clean clay pot (bottom) with evenly moistened vermiculite, perlite, or sand. Treat ends of cuttings with a root-promoting powder, if desired. Insert bare stem ends in rooting medium. Water and keep in cool, light location.

After three weeks, remove a cutting to check root development (top). Time needed varies, but it shouldn't take more than five or six weeks to produce roots of the size shown—large enough to transplant to a separate pot.

For newly rooted cuttings (center) choose pots not over 4 inches in diameter. Supply bottom drainage. Spread roots as you fill with standard potting soil mixture. Water well and keep away from sun for the first few days.

If cuttings show a tendency to wilt (bottom), enclose the pot and stem cuttings in a plastic bag during the rooting period. Use a rubber band to hold the bag in place. It's easily removed when you need to water the plant.

Leaf cutting

Such familiar house plants as African violets, gloxinias, and a number of begonias bear leaves that are capable of producing roots. In the case of the smaller-leaved plants whose leaves are borne on stems, the entire leaf is used for propagation. For the larger-leaved plants, each leaf must be cut into several sections for rooting, as pictured and described on this page.

Cover a jar or glass (below) with foil or wax paper. Pierce holes to accommodate the leaf stems. In water, roots form in three to four weeks—more rapidly than in sand, vermiculite, etc.—but are brittle and break easily.

When roots are well established (bottom)—like those pictured, transfer rooted cutting to an individual pot, using standard potting soil mixture. New growth will arise in a few weeks and the original leaf will eventually wither.

Big-leaved begonias and some other plants can be rooted from leaf sections (top). Cut leaf apart so that each unit includes a part of the main stem. Cut off tip of each section in order to reduce problems of wilt during rooting.

Insert base of leaf sections in sand, vermiculite, or perlite (middle). About ⅓ of cutting should be submerged. Check root formation after two or three weeks, and when it is sufficient, pot each section individually in a 2- or 3-inch pot.

Another kind of leaf sectioning (bottom) may be done with prominently veined leaves. Cut a 1-inch stem with leaf and insert it in rooting medium. Anchor leaf, face up, with toothpicks. Sever each main vein. Cover pot with plastic.

Root division

Division is one of the least complicated ways to increase a collection of house plants. It consists merely of separating an existing plant into two or more sections, then potting each part individually.

Any plant that grows in clumps and that has a separate root system for each of its parts below the surface of the soil can be divided into two or more portions. Whenever a plant belonging to this group is in need of repotting, decide whether to shift it to a bigger pot or to divide it.

The decision ought to be based on the appearance of the plant—whether it has an 'overgrown' look—and its comparative size in relation to its surroundings.

Look at plants with an eye to their needs (below). Do they need dividing? The two plants at right are just reaching an attractive size; they won't benefit from dividing. The three at left will look and grow better after dividing.

To remove plant from pot (top) turn it upside down. Give pot rim a sharp tap on the edge of a table, supporting plant with one hand. Soil ball (if uniformly moist from watering the previous day) will slide out easily.

Shake the soil from the roots (middle) so you can see where stems join the main plant. Select points for cutting only where each section will have good roots of its own. Pull sections apart gently and sever with a sharp knife.

Plant new sections (bottom) in the same way as for any house plant. Use a standard potting soil mixture, firming it around the roots. Water thoroughly and keep the newly potted division out of the sun for a few days.

Runners/offsets

Those house plant oddities that send out aerial runners and form new plantlets and ready-to-grow roots at the end of each runner are a cinch to propagate. Grown in a natural setting, the weight of each developing rosette will bring it down until it is in contact with moist soil, after which it quickly develops roots. Propagating these plants is a matter of imitating nature.

The strawberry saxifrage (below) is one of the commonly grown house plants that forms new plants at the ends of runners. To get plantlet to root, just pin the runner onto moist soil in a small pot nearby. Anchor with a hairpin.

Roots will form (bottom) within a few weeks in a soil mixture that's half peat moss and half sand. Keep the soil continuously moist during the rooting period. When plantlet has developed enough roots to be firmly attached, sever.

Air-layering

Some large plants with thick, woody stems drop their lower leaves if grown too long in dim light, or if overwatered. To 'bring them back to earth' and to restore their attractiveness, use the process of air-layering. This is a way of encouraging plants to grow new roots at one of the leaf nodes on the stem section left bare by leaf drop. Follow the pictures and text below.

First step (below) is to cut a lengthwise notch at the point you want new roots. Insert sliver of wood in notch to discourage healing. Use wet sphagnum moss in a sheet of plastic to wrap cut and to supply needed moisture.

In four to five weeks (bottom) moss ball will be filled with new roots. (During this period, check to see that moss stays moist; add water, if needed.) Cut off below roots and pot. Keep watering old plant. New top will sprout.

Index

A-B-C

D-E-F

*Bold numbers indicate pages containing major cultural information.